WRITING WORKS

A manager's alphabet

Krystyna Weinstein

INSTITUTE OF PERSONNEL AND DEVELOPMENT

First published in 1995

Typeset by The Comp-Room, Aylesbury
Printed in Great Britain by
The Short Run Press, Exeter

British Library Cataloguing in Publication Data

A catalogue record for this book is available from the British Library

ISBN 0-85292-577-8

The views expressed in this book are the author's own, and may not necessarily reflect those of the IPD.

INSTITUTE OF PERSONNEL
AND DEVELOPMENT

IPD House, Camp Road, London SW19 4UX
Registered office as above. Registered Charity No. 1038333
A company limited by guarantee. Registered in England No. 2931892

CONTENTS

PREFACE

This book is the result of several years' experience in the running of writing workshops for a number of major UK corporations. Many of the ideas included here are the result of ideas that emerged in the course of those workshops, and several of them were created in collaboration with the participants. We have spent much of our time in the workshops working on the ongoing documents and participants' texts (ie an action learning approach). I would like to thank in particular those whom I have worked with in Raychem and National Power (previously CEGB) for all the opportunities and encouragement they have given me.

Other ideas have emerged as I have become aware of how I myself approach and tackle the writing – and editing – that I do. My aim, in this manager's alphabet, has been to be as straightforward, practical, and helpful as possible. I hope I have succeeded.

London, January 1995

INTRODUCTION

You may be wondering, 'Why another book on writing?' And why in this alphabetical form? Alternatively this may be the first book you've looked at on the subject of writing. Whatever your reason for picking it up, let me explain how it may help you.

Many of us get stuck when we write. We don't seem able to say what we want, or feel uncomfortable and uneasy with what we've already written because it doesn't convey what we wanted to say, nor does it feel like 'us' saying it.

Rather than having to wade through a thick, conventional tome, with the author's ideas structured into chapters, to find out what you could have done differently, or what hints and guidelines the author may have, this alphabetical format allows you to turn to whatever it is you want to be reminded of, or feel stuck on. Entries are signalled by words in CAPITALS.

For instance you might turn to the entries listed under PARAGRAPHS or PUNCTUATION; or you could look at HEADINGS or LOGIC AND LINKING. Alternatively your eye might be caught by DEADLY SINS, RHYTHM AND FLOW, even FEELING STUCK?, or BE YOURSELF – which will remind you of how to write in your own words, with your own energy.

Then again you may want some practical guidelines on how to structure and what to say in c.v.s, memos, or proposals. Some of the more common daily documents that may worry you are described under the appropriate letter of the alphabet.

THE IMPORTANCE OF WRITING

Writing, as one manager said to his staff, needs to be 'transparent'. It needs to flow like water, be easy to follow, and have its own energy and rhythm. Readers should feel they are being guided through a document by its signposting and logic (be it a report or memo). Texts should not make readers stop because they feel lost in a confusion of muddled thinking; or irritated because the texts are full of grammatical and spelling mistakes; readers should not feel unsure why a document has been sent to them, or what they are meant to do with it. Such documents reflect badly not only on the individual writers but also on their departments and even their organisations, if the document is for an external audience.

The written word is the body language of an organisation. It tells a reader not only about the person who has written it (see below) but also a great deal about the organisation that has produced it. Thus, if it is full of mistakes or ill thought-out this might be taken to represent the organisation's, or department's, inability to think. Can you trust them? Can you do business with them? Do their muddled words reflect muddled actions? The language of a document also gives many clues, as do other eye-catching visual details. They all communicate.

As individuals also we are judged by our writing. Not only does it tell our readers about our ability to use language, it also reveals our grasp and understanding of a subject, our ability to understand details, to think clearly, to be aware of readers' needs, even to understand the wider context in which our text will be seen, or the implications of what we are saying. In fact our inability to convey our thoughts in writing to others can – and has – stopped many people from being promoted, from gaining positions they sought.

Maybe it is for all these reasons that writing worries

many people. It is something etched in stone or onto paper or hard disk. It is there for everyone to see. Unlike the spoken word that disappears into the atmosphere, and is transient (unless captured on tape or video!), people can go back to what has been written. They have the time to reread, digest, and comment in depth. Writing involves creating a record for future use.

WRITING ISN'T ALWAYS EASY

To write well is hard work. A well-written document rarely emerges at a first attempt; it may not come easily, in a flash. As Dr Johnson correctly observed some 200 years ago, 'What is written without effort is generally read without pleasure.' Like anything else we learn, to write well takes practice – and time. There are also principles to be followed, models to be used, and good writers to emulate.

Language is a rich and varied thing. It is constantly changing, and being invented. Words exist now that no one had dreamt of even 20 years ago. The English language is particularly rich: while the *Oxford English Dictionary* contains some 500,000 words it is thought that an educated person uses only around 50,000 – a mere tenth of the total.

Business writing doesn't give a writer the scope that fiction does, but it still allows for something less uniform and stilted than much of business writing today.

WRITERS ARE ALSO READERS

Remember that although this book is aimed at you, as a writer, you are also a reader. Your own reactions to others' texts and your evolving documents, and awareness of what you do or don't like in them are a good guide to help you produce better documents yourself!

In my workshops I always ask participants to spend a few minutes doing an exercise answering questions on how they behave as readers: how they read, what irritates them in others' writing, what attracts or repels them. Their answers provide them with further hints on what they, as writers, should avoid doing. Some comments which crop up all the time are:

- too much text on a page, not enough white space, too few paragraphs
- no logic
- too much detail
- bad grammar and sloppy spelling
- difficult writing: complex vocabulary, and sentences that don't flow
- no indication why I've been sent the document, or why I should read it
- no clear indication what the document is about
- boring titles
- too few headings.

After this exercise I also ask participants to think about *how* they read: do they skim, dip in, or hunt for key words and phrases? Simply being aware of this means that as a writer you will begin to create documents that are more reader-friendly.*

HOW TO USE THIS BOOK

You may choose to use this book in its strictly alphabetical form and turn to, say, VERBS to remind yourself perhaps of the

* *An interesting article entitled 'If all else fails, read the instructions' appeared in the* New Scientist *13 June 1992.*

value of using the active form of verbs; or COLOURS OF WRITING, to make sure your texts are fully rounded and helpful to your readers.

Alternatively you may prefer to read the next section (the 'writing cycle'), to have a 'model' of the whole in your mind, and to see where the various bits of this alphabet fit.

THE WRITING CYCLE

Writing consists of a cycle: see Figure 1.

Figure 1
The Writing Cycle

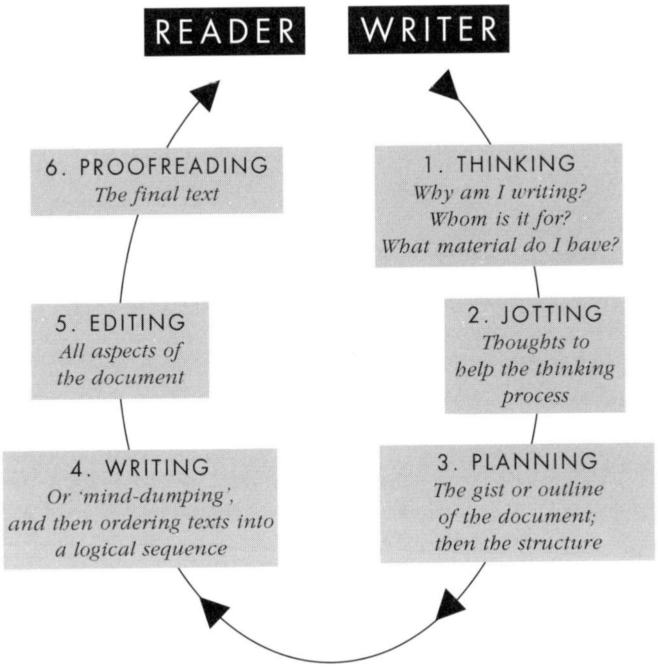

READER
WRITER
1. THINKING
Why am I writing?
Whom is it for?
What material do I have?
2. JOTTING
Thoughts to help the thinking process
3. PLANNING
The gist or outline of the document; then the structure
4. WRITING
Or 'mind-dumping', and then ordering texts into a logical sequence
5. EDITING
All aspects of the document
6. PROOFREADING
The final text

We rarely just sit down and start writing (even if that is what seems to happen!). Our minds will have been doing some thinking before we actually put pen to paper, or finger on keyboard. Even as we write, we are doing more than simply flinging words down on paper. We are going through some process (more or less effectively!) of structuring our thoughts. Once the text is written we then go through – or at least we should – a rigorous editing stage.

If you want to use this book in a systematic way, make a list of the problems you encounter when writing. At what stage of creating a document do they occur? So, a problem such as 'I'm not sure who my reader is' falls into the category 'thinking' (see Figure 1). Without knowing the answer to this you won't be able to write. Similarly if you're not clear about your purpose in writing, or what you hope will be achieved by it, you also won't be able to write. (For more on this, turn to READERS: WHO ARE THEY?, SIX Ws, and WHY ARE YOU WRITING?)

If on the other hand you have problems structuring your thoughts, turn to OUTLINE or MIND MAPS. If you want specific ideas on how to structure a REPORT or MEMO, turn to these entries.

If your problem is not being able to express clearly, in simple English, what you want to say, turn to WRITING IS CREATING, which will give you hints and refer you on to other helpful entries. Try also SAY IT and WRITE LIKE YOU SPEAK; THESAURUS and CHOOSE THE FAMILIAR WORD have some further ideas.

Lastly, if your texts are always heavily altered by someone – your manager? – maybe you're missing out the vital step of EDITING ie becoming the editor and objective reader of your own document, coming fresh to the subject.

Remember: all writing is persuasive. You will persuade readers that your text is the 'best' through the clarity of your thinking, a logical structure, your knowledge of the facts, figures and arguments put forward, the quality of your writing, and the professional appearance of the final document you produce.

QUOTE/UNQUOTE

> “*If language is not correct, then what is said is not what is meant. If what is said is not what is meant, then what ought to be done remains undone.*”
>
> Confucius (551–479 BC)

A

ABBREVIATIONS

Abbreviations are a very useful shorthand. They save us from having to write out a name, title, or long descriptive term each time we refer to it. Abbreviations abound in every organisation, profession, or specialism, and our written, as well as our spoken, language is full of them. They ease and speed up communication.

Where they cause confusion is however when they are used in material written for the uninitiated – for people outside the organisation, profession, or specialism. When you use them for the first time in any document write out the full name, title, or term the first time you use it and put the abbreviation immediately after it within brackets. Thereafter the reader should remember what the various initials stand for!

If you are using a number of abbreviations your reader may become confused (wouldn't you, for instance?) or get irritated because he or she has to go back and try to find what the letters stand for. If you think this may happen put all the abbreviations and the terms they stand for into a glossary of abbreviations at the beginning or end of your document – and tell the reader you have done so, either in an INTRODUCTION or by listing the glossary in the TABLE OF CONTENTS.

ABSTRACT WORDS

Abstract words are those you

can't picture or 'touch'. They are words conjured up purely in the mind, with no concrete reality. As a result they can lead to confusion, since a reader may picture something quite different from what is in the writer's mind! They are useful to help us generalise or to pull ideas together into a whole. But frequently they become so general and abstract as to lose their meaning.

Writing that contains a high proportion of abstract words is difficult to understand, is difficult for a reader to remember, and is in fact inefficient in transferring information, simply because the reader can't visualise what the writer is saying.

Below are some examples of abstract words in frequent use. In many instances they beg the question, 'What exactly do you mean?', or 'Please explain what you understand by . . .':

ability	*enhance*	*problem*
achievement	*environment*	*procedure*
activity	*features*	*purpose*
application	*flexibility*	*quality*
characteristics	*management*	*responsibility*
circumstances	*method*	*situation*
condition	*objectives*	*standpoint*
developments	*position*	*strategies*

On reading an abstract word our first reaction is either to guess what the writer meant, create our own meaning, or admit that we're not sure what is meant. As a writer, be aware of this, and when you use an abstract term give an example of what you mean. So, for instance, if you write a sentence along the lines of:

'The facilities in the building are inadequate'

using two abstract words ('facilities' and 'inadequate') tell your reader what you mean by facilities (the toilets, or the telephone system?) and define what you mean by inadequate (for the disabled, or for the number of people using them?).

Try another example – a fairly typical sentence:

'The lack of communication presents problems'

'Lack' could mean 'none', 'limited' or 'too specialised', or 'of the wrong sort'. 'Communication' could be 'no chance to talk', 'nothing in writing', or 'no meeting'. 'Presents' begs the question 'now?', 'in the future?', 'for whom?', and 'does something need to be done?' – or is this a statement of fact? Lastly 'problems' begs the question 'what sort? – give me some examples', 'who has the problem?', 'are they problems, or rather questions that need to be thought about?', and 'are we looking for solutions?'

On page 84 I've given three possible versions of the sentence: 'If you are expected to produce documents that are clear and well structured and coherently written, the opportunity and environment need to be provided.' This clumsy sentence, however, provides another instance of the use of abstract words: 'environment' and 'opportunity'. Both need to be backed up with examples of what the writer means by them (eg 'environment' may refer to a quiet writing room; 'opportunity' may refer to time being allocated to the task in hand). Without these examples a reader will not be clear what the writer has in mind, and may have different ideas in his or her own mind that could lead to later misunderstandings.

Once you've given some indication of what you have in mind your readers will be able to focus their minds. The reason you need to give this indication is that, obviously, they can't ask you what you mean, as they would no doubt do if you made such a statement in front of them.

Even everyday, simple words can lead to misunderstanding. 'Let's go for a walk', can be misinterpreted as 'a short stroll', 'a long vigorous walk', or 'a day's hike'. Equally it might be shorthand for saying 'we need to talk'. (See MEANING IS IN PEOPLE.)

And how many times has the word 'help' caused misunderstanding, unless you explain what you mean? Are you saying 'I'll do it for you', 'I'll give you some ideas', 'I'll spend some time with you', or maybe even 'I'll give you some money'? Not being clear can lead to misinterpretation, false hopes, and recriminations.

In other words, as a writer you have to do a lot of thinking on behalf of your READERS and anticipate their questions. This, no doubt, is why many people find writing more difficult than speaking. (See CHOOSE THE FAMILIAR WORD; FOG INDEX.)

People who were watching as the *Challenger* space shuttle took off in January 1986 will probably never forget the horror they felt when it blew up. But how many remember the words uttered by a NASA spokesman who, as he watched his monitor go blank, said in a calm voice: 'Obviously a major malfunction.'

I remember standing on a British Rail station some years ago on a winter's day, and being informed by a voice on the loudspeaker system that there would be no trains running 'due to adverse weather conditions'. In fact there were several feet of snow and strong gusting winds over the Pennines – the route of the train. And only recently a mainline station in

London announced that 'the concourse is slippery due to the wet weather conditions . . . Please proceed with caution'. No mention of the downpour outside, or of walking carefully!

There may have been much mirth, similarly, over the 'wrong kind of snow' and 'leaves on the tracks' – but at least we knew what was getting in the way of trains running normally.

Some 50 years ago Hitler claimed, in his own (translated) words, to have lost the Battle of Stalingrad in 1943 'due to unforeseen circumstances'. What he failed to mention was the lack of adequate food, clothing, and ammunition, the too few men, and the atrocious weather conditions. His two chosen words, 'unforeseen circumstances', conveyed nothing.

ABSTRACTS

Abstracts are short descriptions of longer texts – usually reports or articles – for use by library information systems. They most frequently accompany scientific papers, and are no more than 10 lines long. Their purpose is to tell a reader what the document is about. To help with this, they also include a list of key words that will let potential readers decide whether they would find the paper useful.

If you need to write an abstract ask other colleagues what they put in them; alternatively look at a few and follow the example they set.

ADJECTIVES AND ADVERBS

Use adjectives and adverbs sparingly. They can make a real point in any text you're writing. But if you overdo them the text may begin to seem – to a reader – less objective and much more your own, very subjective, judgement. This may of course be what you need to do – or have been asked to do. So you need to judge and be clear what you are aiming to achieve with your text. If subjectivity is called for, then adjectives and adverbs may have their place; if objectivity is called for, use them sparingly.

AGENDAS

Agendas are a list of items to be discussed at a meeting either of a regular committee or group, or of a one-off gathering. It notifies those attending what will be happening, and what they need to think about beforehand or maybe prepare themselves for. The agenda is also the document that the person who writes up the MINUTES will follow.

There are a few conventions about agendas. Obviously they need to state, at the top of the page, what meeting is taking place, where it will take place, and when (date, and times of beginning and end).

Agendas of regular meetings will normally begin with the item 'Present' ie to note in the minutes those present and receive apologies from those unable to attend. The next item is normally 'Minutes of the previous meeting'. This is an opportunity for members to comment on the minutes of that meeting, as reported: do they represent what was said; are there any omissions? The next item is 'Matters arising' ie issues that arise out of those minutes – possibly more information, or future actions to be taken. Quite often these 'matters' are items on the current agenda. A group with its own finances will probably list these on each agenda (but there is no hard and fast rule).

Thereafter an agenda will list the issues to be discussed at the meeting. This list is brief – simply a few words, but enough for members to know what the issues are.

Agendas will be set by the chairperson or 'secretary' to the group, in consultation with other members. The agenda will be sent to all those attending the meeting at least a week beforehand (it will have no doubt been pre-arranged).

AND, BUT, ALSO

Can you start a sentence with 'and' or 'but'? Yes, if you know what you are doing, and why you are beginning your sentence in this way. There's nothing inherently wrong with doing so. But (!) you do need to make sure that the 'and', and what follows, isn't an afterthought that you have simply been too lazy to incorporate earlier into the text. This applies particularly to the word 'also' at the beginning of a sentence: it is usually suspect.

ARGUMENTS, SUGGESTIONS, AND IDEAS

One of your tasks as a writer may be to offer your reader some arguments, suggestions, or ideas on an issue to be decided or an action to be undertaken.

You may not have been asked in so many words to give these elements. You might quite simply have been asked to 'look into *x*' or 'justify the reasons for *y*'. So you may have to read into a request more than seemed to be there at first sight.

If you have been asked to write such a document you can't simply say, 'I recommend' or 'I suggest we do *z*'. You have to justify your thinking and your choice; to show that you have considered other options and rejected them; to show also the benefits of what you are recommending; and to state what will happen if your recommendations are not followed.

Below are a few guidelines on how to structure a text whose focus is on providing suggestions, ideas, or recommendations.

SUGGESTIONS/IDEAS

1. State reason why you are investigating options: what outcome is looked for.
2. Mention existence of a number of options, but that you are recommending one in particular – and will discuss below why this one and not others.
3. State separately – and clearly – for each suggestion/idea:
   - a its advantages/benefits
   - b its disadvantages/drawbacks
   - c in what circumstances it will be particularly good
   - d what will happen if not followed
   - e anything else that should be considered
4. State your preferred suggestion, recommendation, idea
5. State your fall-back position
6. Recommend how to proceed, if agreement is reached.

ARTICLES It is very difficult to make any generalisations about writing articles, for there is no prescribed format for them. But there are some obvious points to bear in mind. An article needs to be written with a specific audience in mind (see READERS). If you are planning to write an article you need also to have identified a few journals that might be interested in seeing it. Armed with this you can then get an idea of the type of piece they are likely to publish.

To be published, articles normally have to make an interesting or unusual point, or describe specific experiences. As with any written piece they need to state clearly at the beginning what their aim is, or what they are about (see FRONTLOADING). Because most printed articles are relatively short they need careful writing and even more careful editing.

Superfluous words and phrases (see FLAGWAVERS) or ideas that aren't directly related to the subject matter should probably be cut out. If you can place HEADINGS throughout the text this will help the editors of the journal or magazine.

If you want an article to be published, write it and send it off. Don't write suggesting you'll come up with one. And don't be disappointed by rejections. It happens to every writer. Try sending the article to another journal or magazine. If those who reject it tell you why they have done so, you may want to have another look at what you've written. Is your message clear? Have you made your points succinctly? Is the piece well written? Would *you* find it interesting and easy to read? Become your own reader!

ASK OTHERS

You may feel that writing is an activity to be undertaken alone. Committees do not usually write good material. So, yes, writing is in the end best done alone. However, asking others to help out, particularly at the thinking and editing stages (see Figure 1), is an excellent idea. None of us has a monopoly on good ideas, and once we have written something it is very difficult to judge it objectively. If you're asking for help at the thinking stage it's probably useful to sort out your own ideas first, or at least formulate some questions, so that others can give their opinions or suggest other ways of approaching the subject you're writing about. So by talking to them you may realise that you haven't really thought through the SIX WS; or when you ask them to read through what you've written they may tell you that your structure isn't very clear. (See LOGIC AND LINKING; STRUCTURE.)

If you're asking a colleague to read through a first draft of your text – to act, in fact, as an editor – they may also comment on your language and on whether the ordering of your thoughts is clear, or whether you have made too many large jumps in your thinking, or expressed yourself too tersely, and lost your reader in the process.

QUOTE/UNQUOTE

"*There is no such thing as failure, only feedback.*"

Anon.

BE YOURSELF

Words, and the way you put them together, convey more than the surface meaning. They convey who you are, your personality. We all speak differently, with different intonation. Our speech conveys a great deal about us. So should our written words. If you feel uncomfortable with what you've written, your readers will sense it.

Being yourself is particularly important if you are being assessed on how well you communicate in writing. Many MCI (Management Charter Initiative) and NVQ (National Vocational Qualification) assessments for competencies now include 'written communication' as one of the skills that people are expected to have. MCI standards on 'informing others' use such phrases as:

- ✦ organising a logical, clear argument that addresses the needs and priorities of recipients in a variety of situations
- ✦ giving information that is current, relevant, and accurate
- ✦ presenting information in a manner and at a level appropriate to the receiver.

Evidence that you have achieved the standards includes producing reports, manuals, newsheets, or articles.

Obviously, being yourself needs to be tempered with common sense. You have to gear what you are writing to your readers and their needs (see WHY ARE YOU WRITING?). Within those limits, however, express yourself with your individuality, as you do when you speak. (See FACTS AND FIGURES; KNOWLEDGE.)

Express, then, your own energy and enthusiasms. Don't be a clone – use your own style! (See WRITE LIKE YOU SPEAK.)

BEGINNINGS

Beginnings of texts and documents are always difficult to write. Because of this we tread carefully, we meander in obliquely, we skirt around an issue before taking the plunge.

Yet beginnings are important. They are the 'come hither' of a document – after the title, that is. How many of us, before buying a novel, read the first sentence to see whether our imagination or interest is caught by it enough to make us go ahead and spend our money?

The same is true of any document: it has to have a strong beginning. Most of us have too much to read. We reach for the document that we think will be the most interesting to read. So how do you begin to write your own, attention-grabbing text?

You could leap in directly with a bold statement in your first sentence; pose a question; confirm your readers' expectations; or make a provocative or unexpected statement. In all instances the first sentence or two should give your readers something to hook onto. They should have a clear notion why they should continue to read the document.

Don't make people hunt for the reason why they should be reading your document somewhere in the middle of the second or third paragraph; or worse still, make them wait till the end of the second or third page before they come to the purpose of the document.

If you don't want to be daring make sure at least you state straightforwardly in your first few sentences the reason for your document and why the person should read it. You may also squeeze in somewhere what you want them to do as a result of reading it. (See FRONTLOADING; INTRODUCTIONS.)

BIBLIOGRAPHIES AND REFERENCES

Bibliographies and references are an important part of many written documents. They either refer your readers to material you have read, and want to draw to their attention, or they are texts which back up statements you have made, and give your document greater credibility.* References may also be a vital part of your document, either because you are doing a follow-up piece, or because your task is to comment on similar, previously written material.

How to refer readers to bibliographies or references is a matter of choice, taste, or following a HOUSE STYLE.

Bibliographies and references may:

- be incorporated into a text, either in brackets next to the particular issue or statement they refer to, or where the writer wants to direct the reader to a text that will elaborate a point
- be listed in footnotes, either at the bottom of the page on which they occur (a practice often used in academic and research texts), or at the end of a section or document. In either case, they need to

* *I initially wrote '. . . draw their attention to . . .' but when I reread the sentence it sounded clumsy. I also remembered that we normally try not to end phrases or sentences with propositions so I altered the shape of the sentence. (See* NEVER ONE WAY*.)*

follow a numbering system. Numbers – usually in small superscript (eg [2]) – are placed in the text, and the same number is used for the reference. If there is only one reference then it may be easier merely to put an asterisk (*) where relevant, and then choose whether the reference will be placed at the bottom of the page or at the end of the section or document.

If the references are to books, then the author, title, publisher, and date of publication need to be given eg 'Joe Bloggs considers this an excellent way of approaching the subject (J. Bloggs, *How to Use a Computer*, Dixon, 1995). If the reference is to an article, then the reference will be 'J. Bloggs, 'How to use a computer', *IT News*, vol. 2, pp. 20–23, 1995). Note the different commonly used way of indicating books, articles, and journal titles. If the reference is to an internal document identify it for your readers and use the same way of distinguishing what sort of reference it is. Reports, in this instance, would be styled in the same way as journals.

A slightly different way of styling bibliographies and references is to give an author's surname first, and place the date of publication after it:

Bloggs, J, (1994). *How to Use a Computer* (Dixon)

Most organisations that produce documents have their own house style which tells writers how to tackle this issue, and hence create a consistent approach.

BRIEFING NOTES

Briefing notes are, appropriately, brief – normally two to three pages long, and are for someone going to a meeting. When preparing them you obviously need to know what the meeting is, what it is that the person you're briefing needs to know (and he or she may not be clear about that!), what role they are playing at the meeting (are they presenting an item, or responding to someone else?), whether they want to emphasise a particular angle, and so on.

You need to think about how such notes will be used at the meeting. Usually they will be on a table, and need to be easy to refer to. So, to be helpful to the reader, the layout needs to allow for space for making notes; should highlight the main issues with bullet points, for the reader to see them at a glance; probably use key words rather than long sentences; and use headings that signpost the reader's way through the two or three pages.

BULLET POINTS

Bullet points have several uses and many advantages. They are a useful way of SIGNPOSTING or HIGHLIGHTING to your reader – and incidentally to yourself, as you write – the main points you're trying to make, or the list of items to which you wish to draw attention.

They further help the reader precisely because they are visually striking. We're drawn, as readers, to visual items in a text, if only as a break from words. For this reason bullet points and other VISUAL MATERIAL can be used to great advantage. But don't overuse them on any one page, or even within an entire text.

The disadvantage of bullet points is that it may be difficult to refer back to the points you have made in them. For instance, when you're discussing your text with a reader, referring to the items listed with bullet points means you have to refer to page numbers, or sections of a text. So, think: would it be easier to put either numbers or letters in the place of the bullet points?

There are no hard and fast rules about how to punctuate

a text in and around the bullet points. The standard way of ending the sentence before the bullet points is to place a colon (:) or full stop there. You may then begin each point (or single word, if that is all you are placing after the bullet points) with a capital or a small letter. Whichever you use, however, be consistent thereafter in the rest of the bullet points. Similarly, you may put some punctuation (a full stop, for instance) at the end of the bullet points, particularly if each was a full sentence. If it was a phrase you need not use any punctuation. But whichever you use, again, be consistent. (See CONSISTENCY; PUNCTUATION.)

BULLETIN BOARD ITEMS

Items for bulletin boards – if they are to be read by anyone passing by – need to be eye-catching. There is little point in producing a small memo-like document meant to be read by one person sitting at a desk.

Bulletin board items, like newspapers, have to aim at catching readers' attention. They need clear, large headings. Those HEADINGS need to be catchy and have some action in them, or even pose a question – that often stops people passing by!

Layout will be crucial. And colour will also help to catch people's eye. Maybe you can use the drawing skills of someone in the office to create an interesting visual effect. Obviously not everything lends itself to this advertising-style of layout, but the more it can pull the eye, the more likely it is to be read.

The words also need to grab readers' attention. The opening sentences will be important (see FRONTLOADING). Like the opening sentences of articles in newspapers or good weekly journals or magazines they will try to encapsulate the ESSENCE of the 'story' that follows.

Items to go on a bulletin board can be written in a more chatty style than, say, formal letters or memos. In this sense they probably resemble E-MAILS. Once you've tried writing in this freer style you may find it tempting to try it out on other documents you have to produce! (See WRITE LIKE YOU SPEAK.)

QUOTE/UNQUOTE

“*To fix something in the memory, it is of great value when we are reading to imprint on the memory the colour, shape, position, or placement of* [*words*].”

12th-century reminder to manuscript writers

CAPITAL LETTERS

Capital letters are used for proper names, place-names, and often, in organisations, names of departments or sections, and people's positions or titles within them. Using capital letters gives a sense of importance.

Too many capitals in a text can however become an irritation to the reader. They also create a sense of formality. When writing, stop to consider whether you really do want to use capital letters for all positions and titles eg 'Personnel Director', or whether 'personnel director' is just as acceptable. Capitals used for all personal titles and roles, as well as all departments and sections, make a text visually very heavy going.

CHOOSE THE FAMILIAR WORD

Something odd happens when we start writing. Our normal, everyday language deserts us and we begin to use words and phrases that we wouldn't use when speaking. We do this, so I'm told, because longer and more complicated words and phrases make our text sound more important.

Somehow the length of words has become associated with the length of time spent producing the document, and complex vocabulary indicates that the text has more 'meat' in it and is obviously 'weightier'.

Long and complex words, many people assume, are impressive. There is a strange belief that by using long words we are showing how educated we are. Many people feel that if they used shorter, simpler words when they write, their documents would not be judged serious or worth reading. Simplicity is equated with being childlike and lacking depth. All of this is, of course, complete nonsense!

Here are some examples of the 'long' contrasted with the 'short', the less familiar contrasted with the familiar. Are the short and the familiar really less worthy? Certainly they are no less correct grammatically.

alteration	–	*change*
anticipate	–	*expect*
assistance	–	*help*
beneficial	–	*helpful*
cognisant	–	*aware*
consequently	–	*so, as a result*
commencement	–	*start*
communicate	–	*tell, write (etc)*
concerning	–	*about*
demonstrate	–	*show*
dispatch	–	*send*
donate	–	*give*
duplicate	–	*copy*
emphasise	–	*stress*
encounter	–	*meet*
endeavour	–	*try*
exhibit	–	*show*
finalise	–	*finish*
frequently	–	*often*
generate	–	*produce*
indication	–	*sign*

initiate	–	*begin*
locality	–	*place, area*
manufacture	–	*make*
merchandise	–	*goods*
methodology	–	*method*
numerous	–	*many*
objective	–	*aim*
obtain	–	*get*
participate	–	*share*
proceed	–	*go*
regarding	–	*about*
requirements	–	*needs*
residence	–	*home*
subsequently	–	*later*
termination	–	*end*
utilise	–	*use*

Many long words, which tend to be nouns, also emerge from perfectly good shorter verbs. One way of avoiding these longer words, which are frequently ABSTRACT WORDS, is to recycle them back into their verbal forms. (See RECYCLING WORDS.)

Obviously texts with vocabulary that is oversimple may turn out to be – and be seen to be – childlike. But there is a balance. Some of the best twentieth-century writers convey their meaning lucidly and beautifully while rarely using long words. Moreover when we speak we tend to use shorter words, unless of course we are trying to impress someone with our erudition!

The English language is immensely rich. It is worth exploiting its breadth to convey our meaning, and using a dictionary and thesaurus to enlarge our vocabulary. But it's a question of balance. (See DICTIONARY; FOG INDEX; THESAURUS.)

CLONING

'Cloning' is not usually tackled in texts on writing, but it is something to look out for. In an attempt to have a consistent style and tone in written material an organisation, or even an individual manager, may inadvertently be creating a stable of clones: a group of people who are constrained to write in a certain way and hence lose their individuality.

Many documents, particularly those produced for outside consumption (for customers, clients, and other bodies), are the external face of an organisation and as such need to have a more or less consistent style, standard, and flavour to instil confidence in those who read them. Documents produced by an organisation are its 'body language'. But an organisation full of clones, whose writing lacks any sense of individuality, also sends readers a message about a certain lack of creativity and originality.

Having to produce documents that rigidly follow a particular style can feel like a death-knell to writers. So if it is your job as a manager of writers to achieve some consistency, be aware that people write best when they can, within reason, be themselves and use their own speech rhythms and ways of self-expression. Texts that lack these components can be very dead and lacking in conviction. This is in turn transmitted to the reader, who frequently becomes bored as a consequence.

COLOURS OF WRITING

A few years ago two authors wrote a book entitled *The Colours of Your Mind.** Their aim was to describe the three 'modes' of thinking that we engage in. What, for me, was relevant in terms of writing was the colour-coding for the different

* *J. Rhodes and S. Thame,* The Colours of Your Mind. *(Fontana/Collins 1988)*

intentions, since a writer needs to be clear about his or her intentions. (See WHY ARE YOU WRITING?) The three colours are red, green, and blue.

Red describes and tells. It denotes information, data, facts, quantities; also insights, impressions, and understanding. This thinking addresses the question: 'Where is the evidence?'

Green searches and realises. It denotes ideas, making connections, lateral thinking, playing with possibilities, as well as inspirations, dreams, and intuition. This thinking builds on the notion of 'Let's try . . .'

Blue evaluates and persuades. It denotes judgements, evaluations, assessments, decisions, and arguments, as well as choices, opinions, and values. It addresses the issue, 'Will it work?' We get things done through blue. It links red and green.

The relevance for writers is this: if you're writing a report, it's not enough to stay in red. You need to move at least into blue, and possibly into green. Red is pure memory. Yet even a certain popular TV programme, where only a regurgitation of red is required, manages to call itself 'Mastermind'. Computers can deal perfectly well with red. What people are paid to do is work on the red to produce blue and green. Blue and green denote the ability to think.

Thus, when asked to write something you need to think: am I being asked for red only, or am I being asked to move into blue and green? Having this colour-coding may help to remind writers who swamp readers with information that this may not be what they've been asked to do – or what they should be doing.

So if your aim is to report on an INVESTIGATION, write a progress report, see what information is available, provide facts and figures, check, categorise, and systematise, you know you can stay in red.

If, on the other hand, you are setting out to find new approaches, discover new possibilities, break out of old habits, challenge, or offer suggestions and ideas, then you will move into green.

If you are asked to form a judgement, give an opinion, assess options, evaluate possibilities, compare, or distinguish between, items, you need to move into blue.

How will you know what is required of you as a writer? Go back to your brief: what have you been asked to write; what is its purpose; what is to be achieved by what you write? (For more on purpose – on the 'why' of writing – see SIX WS; WHY ARE YOU WRITING?)

The value of using colours is that we can apply them to our outlines or 'MIND-MAPS', and place red, blue, or green where required. (For how these colours might apply when you're preparing documents, see INVESTIGATIONS; JOB APPLICATIONS; REPORTS.)

COMPARISONS

If you are using words or phrases that imply a comparison, make sure that the elements being compared are both present in your text. So, if something is 'larger' make sure that your reader knows what it is larger than. If something is to be used 'in a different way', similarly make sure that your reader knows what it is differing from.

Other comparative words that may catch out an unwary writer are: more, less, earlier, later, similar. Often the writer is thinking of what it is that is 'more' or 'earlier' or 'later' than something else but forgets to tell the reader!

CONCLUSIONS

Conclusions are a drawing together of threads. They sum up facts, insights, or judgements in a document. In that sense they should logically come at the end, before recommendations (themselves based on the conclusions). However in many longer documents or reports conclusions are placed near the beginning, because many readers are interested primarily in conclusions and not in the detail of how they were reached (although many need to know in outline how they were reached). (See SUMMARIES; UPSIDE-DOWN REPORTING.)

A conclusion may begin by saying something along the lines of: 'The evidence so far points to . . .'; or 'To draw some conclusions . . .'; or 'The point that we have reached shows us that. . . .'. Each of these phrases draws threads together.

But conclusions can only 'conclude' from what has been said earlier. So make sure that, if you are concluding, you have given your readers the information for them either to draw the same conclusion or a different one! (For more on a typical structure of a report, see REPORTS.)

CONFIDENCE

This may seem an unusual heading to have in a guide on writing, but it's vital to good writing. Just as a lack of confidence can be obvious in the way we speak and behave, it can also show up in our writing.

Confidence will emerge in the language used in the text, in the energy it conveys and the commitment to what is being written. If a writer is not feeling confident the text will be full of 'maybes' and 'mights'. It will not be direct but will meander or use vague, often abstract, words that hide the real meaning.

How do you gain confidence? Well, like most things in life, it comes through practice and through asking for constructive feedback, listening to that feedback, working on the points raised, and practising yet more.

You may find you gain confidence simply by beginning to use the first person in your texts: so, 'I think', 'I propose', rather than 'it is proposed', 'it has been decided' ie trying to WRITE LIKE YOU SPEAK.

You may also begin to feel more confident if you are clear about whom you are writing for, what you want to achieve, and have an OUTLINE in mind. So, turn to SIX Ws and OUTLINE for some ideas and inspiration. (See also BE YOURSELF; FOCUSED FEEDBACK; WRITING IS CREATING.)

CONSISTENCY

'Consistency', said the poet R. W. Emerson, 'is the hobgoblin of little minds.' However, when creating a professional document, consistency is vital.

Inconsistency makes for troubled reading. The reader may quickly become confused or angry, and even begin to focus on such slapdash and unprofessional material rather than concentrate on the content of the document.

You need to ensure consistency of typeface and typesize for the text and for any headings within it. If you change either, you need to have a rationale for doing so, and then be consistent within that. (See HEADINGS; TYPEFACES.)

A consistent layout for all the pages is equally important – it gives the document a professional appearance. Pages should be the same length (as far as possible), paragraph indentations (or lack of) should also be consistent, as should the presentation of visual material, including the naming and numbering – do you call visual material 'Figures' or 'Tables', for instance? And if you opt for both, make sure you know why. Other elements to be aware of are: spelling of names, using abbreviations consistently, creating bibliographies and references – in fact, all the elements of a text!

CONTENTS

(see TABLE OF CONTENTS)

CONVINCING YOUR READERS

In a sense, all writing has this aim: to convince a reader either that you, the writer, know all the facts, have listed all the arguments, have argued all the points fully, and are a reliable source of information.

As writers, we have different ways of convincing. We can convince by:

- ✦ the form of words we use
- ✦ the real energy we place in our text (and not merely the advertising, marketing, or gimmicky sales text)
- ✦ the way we structure our material, so that there is an inexorable logic to what we are saying
- ✦ listing benefits v disadvantages (if they are relevant)
- ✦ drawing on, and referring to, other texts or other people's words.

Written language, like body language, betrays us and our feelings. If we are unconvinced by the arguments we are putting forward, if we are unsure about what we are saying, if we don't fully understand what we are proposing, or if we haven't thought through what we want to say, it will all show up in our writing.

Texts from an unsure or unconvinced writer will bear the hallmarks of woolliness and beating about the bush. This usually shows itself in the form of long sentences, a profusion of abstract and often imprecise words, jumping around the arguments in a disjointed way, meandering through half-developed arguments, glossing over facts and ideas, and dismissing issues too briefly.

Writers need also to remember that words convey not only their own feelings: they also elicit feelings in the reader. Thus if we write of 'problems', a reader's instant, almost subconscious, reaction will be 'oh dear', and a sense of dread or frustration. Drawing attention to a 'problem' is also backward-looking. Better to be looking for solutions, the future, and what you want to be happening. By rephrasing a sentence to talk of what you want to be achieving or doing, and proposing how to get there, rather than resolving 'problems' you will make readers feel more positive and energetic. (See POSITIVE LANGUAGE.)

COPY EVERYTHING

Making copies of everything you write is a necessary and sensible precaution. Texts written on word processors are these days stored on disk and can be easily retrieved. But for quick reference, actual paper copies of shorter documents are often more easily and quickly accessible. Having copies in both forms also ensures that if one source gets lost or damaged you still have the other.

If a text hasn't been written on a word processor, but by hand, then making copies is essential. All you need is to lose your only copy of a piece of material you have slaved over for hours, or even days, to have a sense of complete devastation!

CURRICULUM VITAE – C.V.s

All of us are asked at one time or another to produce a curriculum vitae or c.v. – either when we are applying for a new job or when someone is wondering if we have the background and know-how to do a particular job.

Your c.v. is your work autobiography. It describes you, your interests, and your accomplishments to others in a brief form. 'Brief' means no more than two pages!

C.v.s should begin with your name and address. Standard c.v.s will then give your education – if you have degrees and professional qualifications your school achievements are not particularly relevant. Next, you need to describe your work, starting with your present job and working backwards. In all instances give dates and your title, and who your employer was. Then briefly state what are/were your responsibilities, and your achievements. You may also want to mention any particularly interesting assignments. Say what you did, not simply what your position was. That in itself doesn't tell a reader much.

When listing past jobs go back as far as you feel is relevant. If you have been working for a number of years, and your first job bears no relationship to what you are doing now, you do not have to describe it in detail. One way of dealing with jobs that don't relate directly to the work you are currently doing is to place them together in a category introduced by a phrase such as 'Before *x* I also . . .'.

Remember also that each c.v. should be tailor-made for the job you are applying for. Don't just send the same old c.v. to everyone. For each job you will need to reword your c.v. slightly – possibly emphasising some experiences more than others – simply because that is what the person reading it will be interested in – and will look for.

If you're responding to an advertisement it's useful, before you reword your c.v., to note the key words in the advertisement, and the experience, skills, or the potential that a new employer is seeking. Then look honestly at your own achievements. If you can, use some of those key words – honestly – to indicate what you have done and achieved; that will show the reader you have thought about the work he or she is advertising. Obviously you must not invent what you haven't done, or talk of skills you don't have. If you are called for an interview any untruths will be rapidly detected!

C.v.s need to be laid out with dates and job titles highlighted. To create a neat text that a reader can skim through, dates are often placed in a left-hand column, with the text aligned neatly in a right-hand one.

An alternative way is to bunch together particular jobs or skills you have under appropriate headings. You may then decide whether you will follow a chronological listing or describe your accomplishments in some other way.

Whatever you decide to do, make sure the reader can grasp it quickly and easily, and can follow the logic you have applied to your c.v. (See JOB APPLICATIONS.)

QUOTE/UNQUOTE

> “*It makes one's task easy, one's success likely, if one knows the character of one's correspondent, to get used to his invidious mind, to know what he will gladly hear and what one may properly say to him.*”
>
> Petrarch (1304–74)

DEADLY SINS

The deadly sins of sloth, gluttony, pride, despair, and contempt are known to many writers.

Sloth is when you can't find the energy to start – you delay until the last minute. Though some people write best when under pressure sloth is often a sign of lack of interest or commitment. This may be because you are writing about some work you have finished and, having completed it, you feel it is a step back into the past to relive the action or experience. One way to avoid this is to write notes as you go along which can then be pulled together and edited. Alternatively create an OUTLINE on which to construct the final document; this way you won't have to rely on memory or odd scraps of paper.

Sloth resulting from lack of energy may also be connected with fear: fear that what you write won't be up to scratch, or will be pulled apart by a boss or senior person. If sloth is the result of this (and only you, the writer, really know the cause!) then you may find it useful to look at the entries under WRITING IS CREATING and OUTLINE to begin to give yourself more confidence.

Gluttony is about wanting to put into what you are writing everything you know about the subject. If this is one of your sins, think about why you want to stuff your text as full as possible. Is it to show off how much you know? Remember, your reader has a particular reason for reading your document, and you have a particular reason for both writing and sending it. Being clear about these reasons will in turn give you some idea of what is relevant and what is not.

Your main reason for writing is to express, not impress. On the other hand if you want to impress someone you will do so by being very clear about your purpose and their needs, and writing them a focused document. Showing how much you know may overwhelm rather than impress them. And your inability to focus on the purpose of the document will be judged accordingly, regardless of how much you know.

Pride, another deadly sin, is to do with seeking perfection: either perfection in the sense of not knowing when to stop gathering data, or of never being happy with what you write. Aiming at excellence is crucial; yet seeking perfection may be impossible, not to mention time-consuming. Set your standards high, but be pragmatic also.

Despair is also a common sin: despair that the material will ever fall into place or make sense; that you will express yourself clearly; or that what you are writing is really 'you' – it all sounds and feels as if someone else is doing the writing.

To take the last point first: if this is what is worrying you, scrap what you have written and start afresh by asking yourself, for each sentence initially, 'What am I trying to *say*?'; and then say it in your own words. You'll find that a lot easier than trying to write something that doesn't sound like you.

Despair that what you're writing will ever make sense is likely to arise if you're not really sure yourself what you want to say. Again, stop and ask yourself: 'What am I trying to *say*?' That may begin to clear your mind, until you are sure what you want to say. Writing it then becomes a lot easier.

Remember: woolly thinking = woolly writing.

Alternatively, despair that is the result of being unable to express exactly what you want to may arise because you don't have the appropriate language. A dictionary or thesaurus may help. You may also find that asking colleagues to help you find the exact words or phrases, or seeing how others have expressed themselves in similar documents, makes writing easier.

Lastly, despair because the material won't fall into place may be overcome by going back to your OUTLINE. Write down or draw the parts of it, sketch in the links, and put key words down to help you 'see' the logic.

Contempt is the sin of thinking that what you've written needs no revising or revisiting once it's down on paper or screen. It is up to your reader to make sense of what you've written. Moreover it's up to your reader to unravel your unstructured, unthought-out text, or to hunt out in a morass of meandering sentences what you're actually trying to say.

Contempt will not endear you to your readers. If you can't be bothered to think out what you're saying, and the reason for saying it, then why should your reader spend precious time and effort trying to decipher it?

Finally, what appears to be contempt may, of course, be simple laziness.

DICTIONARY

A dictionary is essential. It will help with spelling (if you don't have a spellcheck on your word processor). It means you can check the word you are using is precisely the one you want, or whether you are using a particular word appropriately.

By using a dictionary you also expand your own vocabulary, and that in turn makes your writing more varied and hence more interesting.

English has an extremely rich vocabulary; yet on an everyday basis an average person uses only a tiny proportion of it. To help expand your own vocabulary, check in a dictionary any words you come across that you don't understand. (See THESAURUS.)

DOS AND DON'TS

- ✦ Do remember what trips you up when you read – and don't make the same mistakes when you write!
- ✦ Do use active verbs rather than the passive form.
- ✦ Do use a dictionary to make sure you're using words appropriately; and a thesaurus, to expand and vary your vocabulary.
- ✦ Do use familiar phrases and words rather than unnecessarily complex, longer ones.
- ✦ Do use headings as signposts for your readers – and for yourself.
- ✦ Do make sure your document is clearly laid out and visually appealing.
- ✦ Don't write to impress; rather, write to express.
- ✦ Don't write in a style that feels unnatural to you; readers will spot it and feel uncomfortable too.
- ✦ Don't write for yourself; write for your readers.
- ✦ Don't make the reader hunt for the essence of what you're writing about, or the actions you are proposing, or the outcomes/results you hope to achieve. Put them 'upfront' – in an opening statement – in whatever you are writing. Every document is written for a particular reason.

EDITING Editing is the last but one stage of writing (see Figure 1). It is often missed out or muddled up with the fourth, writing, stage.

There are several purposes to editing:

- ✦ to see the document as a whole. We often write bits of texts at different times, and may lose track of its total sense.
- ✦ to see the text through a reader's eyes. This is not easy. We become attached to our words and are so close to the text that we can't see it objectively. We also know our subject matter well, and can't see the gaps, or bits that aren't clear. To be able to edit your own text well – particularly if it's a long one – you need to give yourself at least a day's break after writing. Even if it's a letter or memo, taking a short break doing something else will make editing easier.
- ✦ to check that the text flows logically from sentence to sentence and paragraph to paragraph. Would you, as a reader, find it well-composed, comprehensible, satisfying? Are there jumps in thinking or logic that you don't follow? If you have the slightest doubts, you're undoubtedly right!
- ✦ to check the grammar and spelling. Mistakes in either of these may – indeed often do – distract a reader from concentrating on your content. The reader

begins to question your ability, your trustworthiness. If you can't get such simple things as spelling and grammar correct the reader may (rightly or wrongly) begin to suspect your ability to think clearly. In the end the reader may even stop taking in your points and simply look for errors!

- ✦ to rewrite clumsy sentences and phrases, or to cut out 'padding' and FLAGWAVERS – those often unnecessary words and phrases that we often think improve our texts. They do, if their purpose is to create a link with what has just been said, or to take a reader off onto another tack. Shorten long sentences, and make sure paragraphs aren't too long. (See PARAGRAPHS, SENTENCES.)

A useful way to do this part of the editing is to speak out loud what you are reading ie not literally by speaking, but by mouthing or whispering. Your colleagues may wonder if you've taken leave of your senses, but it's a useful test to see whether what you've written sounds right and flows well. Whether you're reading your own or someone else's work, you're likely to have a split-second feeling that something isn't quite right. When you get that feeling, stop and look at the piece of text. Your reaction means there is indeed something not quite right.

- ✦ to check the consistency of: the use of capital letters, abbreviations, typesizes and typefaces of headings of similar weight (see HEADINGS), layout and styling of paragraphs, quotations, references and footnotes, including any numbering system used etc.
- ✦ to take a critical look at the titles and headings: does the title invite the reader, does it tell him or her what the document is about? Do the headings bring the piece alive or are they 'deadheads'? (See HEADINGS.)

- to think about the layout: if you are doing the final document yourself on a word processor check that there is enough space between paragraphs and that it is consistent. Check that page lengths are approximately the same. Make sure there is enough white space on a page.
- to ensure that figures or tables are near to the relevant text. Check the titles and numbering of figures and tables, again for consistency and sequencing. Check that references in the text agree with the titles and numbering.

Some editing can be done on screen – if you are using a word processor. But in the end, to see what a text is really like, you need to edit on paper. I don't know why it is, but you see more when you look at a printed piece of paper than when the text is on screen.

If you have handwritten your material do the editing once it has been typed out. It's surprising how much better you see things when the material is in printed form.

Although you may do some editing as you write (eg rewriting sentences because they sound clumsy) don't as a rule edit as you write. If you do, you may lose your thread. Your creativity gets stopped when you edit because editing isn't about creativity but about 'production'. So: write, and then go back, maybe at the end of a section or a few pages.

One advantage of being aware of these various elements of editing is that when you ask someone else (maybe your boss) to read your material in order to give you comments, and they say something like, 'I don't think this is very good', you can ask them to be specific: is it the logic, the structure, the writing, the layout? Such questioning forces people to give you constructive feedback. The same applies when someone asks you to read through their document. By focusing on the various aspects of editing, you will be able to give others more constructive and helpful feedback.

One final word to would-be editors of other people's work: don't rewrite words, phrases, or sentences merely because you would have written them differently. Every sentence or idea is capable of being expressed in numerous ways. Your way isn't the only or the best one. Correct and rewrite only where the meaning is genuinely unclear, or the writing is truly clumsy. Remember: each of us speaks, and hence will write, in a different way, using our own voice. This makes for interesting reading. And in the end the most important person is the reader for whom the text is being produced! (See PROOFREADING.)

ELEGANCE

This is not so irrelevant an entry as it may at first appear. Elegance in writing is what makes a text both easy and pleasurable to read. It has RHYTHM AND FLOW. The words are well chosen, the sentences are varied in structure and length, and the text conveys something of the writer's personality.

I've been told that this is not achievable in business writing. I disagree. I think it is, though obviously not to the degree that it is in literature. But language is flexible, words exist to be played with, and there are many models to follow in good literature.

E-MAIL

E-mail – an increasingly popular way of communicating – is essentially a memo or letter on screen. It is also often used as an alternative to the telephone. Maybe it is this aspect of E-mails that makes writers feel free to be more relaxed, informal, more 'themselves', when writing them. It may also be something to do with feeling that something written on screen is not as durable as something written on paper.

How you write an E-mail may depend on whether you are viewing it as an alternative to the telephone; or whether it is simply a memo or letter, but in another medium. If it is the former, you may find you will write more like you speak, and feel OK about it! If it is a memo or letter, there is – as this book keeps pointing out – no reason not to write them, too, in a more conversational style.

No matter which form of communication you are 'replacing', the same thinking and planning rules apply as when you're writing paper MEMOS or LETTERS, or speaking to someone on the phone. You still have to tell the reader why you're writing to him or her, and what you hope will be achieved by it.

E-mail, and the greater sense of freedom when writing it, may in fact prove to be one more nail in the coffin of all the unnecessarily formal and long-winded writing that so many organisations appear to require when letters, reports, or other paper-bound documents are created!

ENERGY

Put energy into everything you write. Don't make what you write sound like a limp handshake feels. Use words that convey precisely what you mean (a dictionary or thesaurus will help); use the active form of VERBS; don't meander into sentences – go straight in, without FLAGWAVERS. Be convinced about what you are saying. Put yourself into it, as far as you can. It will show in the energy of what you write. (See RECYCLING WORDS; SENTENCES.)

ESSENCE

The essence, as the word implies, is the distillation of the main point of what a document, or a section of it, is about.

The essence of a document or section may often be put in one opening sentence. In this sense it follows what many well-written newspaper articles do: they put the essence of a story in the opening paragraph, often no more than one or two sentences long. This essence is not a SUMMARY, which tends to be a short version of each part of a document.

To help you arrive at this essence think of the reader who asks him- or herself (probably subconsciously) when picking up a document: 'What is this about, and why am I being sent it? What do I need to do?' Capturing this at the beginning of a document is important. (See FRONTLOADING.) Then you can go into the history, the background, and all the other details (but only if they are relevant).

As an exercise, check the documents you send out or the ones you receive for the following: where is the essence, how long does it take before you get to it, and where is it once you've found it?

Writers often find that the main point they're trying to make – the essence – is stated at the end of sentences rather than at the beginning. Similarly the essence of PARAGRAPHS is often in the last sentence. This is because we were trained, when learning to write essays at school or college, that we have to build up to our main point or findings.

However, for business writing, the reverse is needed (see UPSIDE-DOWN REPORTING). To extract the essence you may find that you have to move the last paragraphs in sections, or even the last sentences in paragraphs, to the beginning – to 'frontload' (see FRONTLOADING). One of the great advantages of the word processor is that moving material around a document in this way is relatively easy.

EXPRESS RATHER THAN IMPRESS

A great deal of corporate writing aims to impress, and not express. When we fall into the trap of trying to impress we begin to use inappropriately long, formal words; our sentences grow longer and contain a greater number of passive verbs; and we risk becoming long-winded and pompous. In general, texts written to impress need a great deal of EDITING!

So why do we produce such texts? A participant on a writing course thought about this and came up with the following reply: '. . . because the weightier the words, the weightier your argument.' In other words by stating your message or idea simply, in everyday language, you wouldn't be able to convince your readers that you had really done a great deal of work or thinking about your subject; long words and complex sentences would make it more convincing – or so this argument goes.

Yet when I ask people what sort of writing they prefer to read, almost everyone says: 'clear, well-expressed texts written in a straightforward style.' So why does everyone write in the long-winded way? 'Because that's what everyone else wants,' comes the response. This sounds like a case of total confusion! (See CHOOSE THE FAMILIAR; FOG INDEX; RECYCLING WORDS.)

FACING YOUR FEARS

Many people are afraid of writing – for a whole lot of reasons. If you are such a person, you are not alone! Sharing your fears, facing up to them, and telling others about them may result in two things:

- ✦ You find others have the same fears, and a fear shared is a fear halved.
- ✦ By talking out loud about the fear you may make it disappear. This may sound nonsensical, but it isn't. It's as though part of our fear is about simply admitting to the fear. Having removed that block we can then use our energy (which before was being used to fight the fear) to work for us.

FACTS AND FIGURES

All texts and documents contain facts and figures. Even if the document you are writing is dealing with ideas these have to be firmly based in an assessment of facts and figures. Whenever you give facts and figures make sure you are confident they are correct. Check them against written sources so that you can point to where they came from and justify your use of them.

If you are trying to make a case for or against something, you do not always need to list every single point. Choose the most powerful ones, those that your reader will understand and be most interested in. Often three or four points make a case as strongly as a dozen. Remember also that your text needs to be geared to particular readers' needs and interests. If you want your readers to remember certain points especially then give them prominence. Repeat them, if necessary. Repetition, provided it isn't overdone, is a good form of emphasis.

Alternatively, highlight them in some way. If you're listing a lot of facts BULLET POINTS make them stand out. If you want to give figures think seriously about some visual way of presenting them – maybe a graph or pie chart. (See HIGHLIGHTING TEXT; VISUAL MATERIAL.) If you are giving a whole mass of figures you may find they interfere with the text. You may then decide to place such material in an appendix to your document. (See KNOWLEDGE.)

FEELING STUCK?

'I don't know where to start'; 'I feel frozen'; 'I've tried writing the introduction and I can't get going . . .' Just three cries of woe! If you do feel stuck and can't get started, there are a number of ways of getting around this block:

- Start writing the part of the document or text that you feel happy with, know best, or that you can express easily. Once you have started you will probably find that other ideas start crowding in.
- Start writing anything, even such sentences as 'I can't start, I feel stuck, I don't know what to write, because I'm not sure whether . . .', and so on. The very act of beginning to write and to think about writing often releases the block, and as you find yourself making some comments on what you have to write, the ideas start flowing.

- Talk into a tape recorder: pretend there is someone listening to what you have to say. Saying what you want to write often releases the block.
- Call your text something different. The word 'report', for instance, often conjures up negative images in our mind – we feel unable to write a 'report'. If that's the case try writing 'my thoughts on . . .'. Just calling the document you have to write by another name often gives you a different appraoch to writing it!
- Go for a walk or get up and make some coffee. (I go and talk to the cat, or do a few minutes' gardening!) Just stopping the mind from working in the same unfruitful groove and giving it a break allows it to find another path to follow.
- Write out the GIST of what you want to say, no matter how short. This then gives you the main elements to expand on in more detail for a longer document.
- Start drawing a MIND-MAP with key words and arrows. A visual stimulus may give you inspiration, for you are engaging the right side of the brain, with its power to make connections and draw on your intuition.

(See THE GIST; MIND-DUMPING; THINK; WHERE TO START?; WHY ARE YOU WRITING?)

FLAGWAVERS

Flagwavers are phrases that start a sentence and announce something rather than going straight to the point. Examples of flagwavers are:

'It must be mentioned that . . .'

'As we have already said . . .'

'It is appreciated that . . .'

'It is of interest to note that . . .'

'As is well known . . .'

'It is not necessary to stress the fact that . . .'

'It is generally agreed that . . .'

'For obvious reasons . . .'

'It is true to say that . . .'

Such introductory phrases may of course serve as links to what has been previously said. But in many instances they are 'padding' or a drift into a sentence that would often sound, and read, better with these phrases deleted. A good editor will spot them and use a red pen on them!

FOCUSED FEEDBACK One of the best ways of improving your writing is to get focused feedback (another is to read good writers). And if you give feedback to someone else on their writing they'll improve, too. It is the only way for a writer to learn.

Feedback may take the form of writing in the margins, giving verbal comments, or (as I often do) ringing places where I find myself stopped by something – anything – in the text that interferes with its flow. It may have made too great a jump for my thought processes to follow; it may be unclearly phrased and have lost its meaning; or there may be a grammatical mistake.

When I give feedback, I first ask the writer to see if he or she can see what it is that has stopped me . . . and they usually can. Spotting your own errors is the first step in becoming a good editor of your own work, and ultimately a better writer!

Focused feedback is something that managers or bosses need to do if their staff are to learn. How can a writer know what to improve, and do differently, if they haven't been told precisely what the reader finds difficult to understand or follow? I have come across many participants in writing workshops who say their managers never tell them precisely either what they liked or found needed changing in their texts. The good bits are ignored; the bad are crossed out and, often, rewritten.

If you want feedback ask for it. And if, when you're given it, you find it isn't specific enough, persist. Ask exactly what was 'wrong' (see EDITING for elements of specific feedback). Should you currently be getting no feedback it may still be worth finding out whether you are providing what your readers need. Could your documents be in any way made more readable?

Similarly give other writers feedback on what you receive from them. Although in some instances it might be politic to ask them whether they want it, if you receive something that is unclear or just incomprehensible you need to tell the writer (if he or she can be contacted, of course).

FOG INDEX

How readable is your writing? Obviously some texts are fine for children, others for Ph.D.s; some for specialists, others for the layperson. There are several ways of 'measuring' or assessing the readability of your texts, and whether they are appropriate for your readers.

The Fog Index – just one of these ways – is based on the number of polysyllabic words and long SENTENCES you have in a particular text. It is these that, between them, make for difficult or easy reading. The Fog Index does not assess the logic of a text, merely its instant readability, and hence the effort someone needs to exert before understanding what he or she is reading.

Such a measure, while useful for any writer, is particularly so for scientists and professionals. Both groups often have many polysyllabic words in their everyday vocabulary and JARGON, so their texts are inevitably going to be weighed down by long words. Each long word, even ones known to the reader, takes up slightly more energy to absorb and translate in the reader's brain. They thus make the reader work harder, and risk losing their goodwill. If your readers have a pile of reading to get through (as most do), you should aim to help them as much as possible.

If your readers – who may know you, and receive documents from you on a regular basis – build up a negative attitude to your writing you risk your documents being prejudged or, worse still, not being read. Think: what do *you* do when you receive a text from someone who, you know from experience, writes badly? So if the subject matter you write about has a large number of long and obscure words try in particular to 'wrap' around them simpler and shorter words.

FOG INDEX

Long sentences, big words, and abstract terms make for heavy and difficult reading.

1 To find your Fog Index, take a sample of at least 100 words of your text.
2 Count the average number of words per sentence; treat independent clauses (such as this!) as a separate sentence.
3 Count the number of 'polysyllables' (words with *three* syllables or more) per 100 words. Don't count words beginning with capital letters; combinations of short and easy words (eg manpower, insomuch); or verbs made into three syllables by adding -es or -ing (eg approaches, incoming). Do, however, count nouns or adjectives with the suffix -ing.
4 Add the average number of words per sentence to the polysyllable count and multiply the sum by 0.4 (ignore digits after the decimal point in the resulting figure).
5 Any material showing a count of 15 or more may be 'difficult' for people who have not been through higher education.

The Fog Index in the table on page 46 will help you to work out a score telling you how 'difficult' your text is. The scores that an adult should aim to have when writing to other reasonably knowledgeable readers is 15–18. If you score less, that is fine; if more, there is a danger that you are making the reader work too hard. A higher score probably means you have SENTENCES with 30–40 words in them; each sentence of such length can easily be broken up into two or more perfectly acceptable, and often clearer, sentences.

A higher score also means that your texts have a large number of polysyllabic words, which make for harder reading, primarily because many of them are ABSTRACT WORDS whose meaning isn't always clear.

FOOTNOTES

(see BIBLIOGRAPHIES AND REFERENCES)

FRONTLOADING

Frontloading means stating at the very beginning of a document one of the following: your purpose; what you hope to achieve by sending your document; the main findings of some work you have been doing; and so on. Frontloading is a way of catching your readers' attention so that they will know, at the outset, what 'journey' they are being taken on.

How many of us, before we buy a book, look at the first sentence to see if it 'grabs' us? The same is true of the everyday material we produce at work. Making it eye-catching for a reader, who already has too much to read, will only help your cause.

Frontloading may take the form of stating an eye-catching detail, an action that needs to be undertaken, or an outstanding result. Whatever you choose to place in that eye-catching opening position, state it in a forceful sentence that goes straight to the point rather than meandering around.

If you become aware that you are meandering into a sentence, stop and ask yourself: 'What am I trying to say?' If you feel unable to frontload a document (be it a memo, letter, or something longer), ask yourself: 'What is the outstanding item, issue, concern, or action raised in the document?' Do you want your readers to do something or respond in some other way? Whatever it is you want, say it upfront eg 'We need to . . .', I'd like to . . .'. This may also help you to find a good title or, if you're writing a memo, a good action-laden HEADING.

To see what I mean about frontloading read the opening sentences of newspaper articles or pieces written in publications such as *The Economist* or *New Scientist*. The gist of the story is always in the opening few sentences. (See also UPSIDE-DOWN REPORTING.)

G

THE GIST Getting down the gist of what you want to say – maybe in a shorthand dozen sentences or so covering the whole subject matter – is a very useful way of beginning to create an outline and structure. Often, when faced with a longer piece to write, we think, 'I haven't got anything to say . . . it'll all fit onto only one page, and that's not enough.' And indeed it may not be.

However, writing out the gist is a start to creating an outline. All the main points you write down in the gist become potential sections to be built on and added to. They are, if you like, overall headings. As you begin to expand on the various points you have made in this shorthand form you begin to create a longer and more rounded text, until you realise you have the makings of a report, article, or other document. (See OUTLINE.)

GRAMMAR Grammar is something many of us were taught in schools but, by and large, have now forgotten. We somehow manage, for the most part, to speak grammatically, and even write grammatically, but we may not be able to put names to the bits of language we are using, or know why they are correct!

Sometimes, however, we get the grammar wrong: we use singular nouns with plural verbs; we create 'sentences' without verbs in them (which means they aren't in fact sentences); we use hanging participles; and we punctuate wrongly, which can result in misleading or nonsensical sentences.

If you have a problem with grammar you may find it useful to buy a simple book on the subject or attend a basic short course to remind you of the principles. Alternatively you can make a habit of reading well-written material so that you begin to notice *how* those authors or journalists write. It means becoming truly aware of what you are reading. (See PUNCTUATION.)

GUT FEELINGS

Be aware of your gut feelings when you write. If your gut tells you that what you're writing isn't clear you can be sure it is correct. If it tells you that you need to write more about some aspect of your subject, that you haven't done it justice – again, your gut will invariably be right. On various occasions I've not reacted to my gut feelings about bits of text I'm writing, only to find that someone reading or editing my text pinpoints precisely those places and says there is indeed a problem: they felt a sentence wasn't clear, they needed more evidence, I'd missed out some step in the discussion, I wasn't convincing, and so on.

Participants on workshops confirm this need to trust gut feelings. They often remark that where I have ringed some part of their text because it stopped the easy flow of my reading they had also had doubts but chose to ignore them!

H

HARD WORK Dr Johnson said that 'What is written without effort is rarely read with pleasure.' He was right. If a document is to be interesting, readable, worth picking, reading through and enjoying, and offer satisfaction to the readers without excessive effort on their part, then the writer will need to put in a great deal of hard work. If you skimp, it will show. The document will look untidy, half-finished, unedited.

'But we don't have time to spend on such details!' is the cry I frequently hear. True, time is precious. However, I have three responses to this:

- The more you practise initially, the quicker and easier writing becomes. In fact it eventually becomes second nature to think about all the issues discussed in this book as you produce a document, no matter which stage you're working on.
- If you are aware that you (and your organisation, department, or section) are judged by the content and appearance of your documents then it is probably worth spending time on them! It may save you time trying to retrieve your reputation later.
- Not spending time now usually means having to find time later, anyway.

HEADINGS Headings help! In a text they are like signposts on a road: they tell your reader of the journey through the text. But they also help you when you're writing.

If you're unsure of what you're trying to say, write a heading that gives its essence. You can do this for simple thoughts that may need only one or two sentences, or for longer chunks of text. Alternatively if you have already written a few sentences or a couple of PARAGRAPHS, but they don't seem to be as clear as you had hoped, try putting a heading, or more than one, above what you've written. It's an excellent test to see which part of a text you have written belongs where, which bits need to be amalgamated, and what is missing.

There are different ways to approach the creation of headings for your readers. A heading may be the ESSENCE of what is to follow; it may pose a question that follows on from what you have written previously, and that your reader will probably have in his or her mind. For this reason a heading that poses a question is often eye-catching.

Headings, like texts, should have movement in them; they should be action-oriented. Headings with verbs in them, or that begin with a 'how' or 'what', have a sense of action which makes them more interesting than 'deadheads' – ones that don't really tell you what is going on. One warning sign that you have produced a deadhead is if you have a heading or TITLE with more than four nouns strung together and no preposition or verb mingled in with them.*

How many headings do you need? How long is a piece of string? There is no one answer. Enough to help your reader, is probably the only helpful answer. Think of headings, as we've already said, as signposts. (See SIGNPOSTING.)

* *In a slightly different context elsewhere in this book I have used the phrase 'our ability to think and act'. The first words I wrote down, however, were 'our thinking and operating ability'. The former is, I think, more precise and easier for a reader to follow. The latter, because of its participial adjectives, is marginally more complex.*

Just as there is a hierarchy of signposts on the roads – blue for motorways, green for main trunk roads, and white for local roads – so headings have a hierarchy. Main headings will be in one typeface and probably be in capitals, and in **bold**. The next 'level' of heading will be in smaller typesize and may only have a capital letter for the first word; a third level of heading may be in *italics*, and so on. (See TYPEFACES AND TYPESIZES.)

It is important to be consistent about the level you give to headings, so that they introduce material of a similar level of importance. In other words, you work with a hierarchy of both texts and headings. One way of helping you decide on the appropriate level is to use (or turn to) your MIND-MAP, which will show you the relative levels of your texts and hence headings. (See TITLES.)

HIGHLIGHTING TEXT

The need to highlight text arises from the way many of us read. We don't necessarily read every page of any document. In many instances we browse, skim, search, or dip in. To help readers do each of these, you can:

- put words in **bold** or *italics*
- indent text
- use bullet points to itemise your thoughts (as I am doing here!)
- create space around the 'special' text by separating it out from the main text
- placing it in a 'box' or table
- use headings.

A text needs SIGNPOSTING in this way to help readers.

HOUSE STYLE House style is the term for the particular way that your organisation wants written material to appear. House style will normally cover such things as:

- how to abbreviate: do you, for instance, write US, USA, or U.S., U.S.A.?
- when to use capitals: for people's positions (Personnel Director or personnel director), or for departments and sections. (A note of caution: too many capitals are distracting and make the text look very formal. Many of them are also plain unnecessary.)
- whether to single- or double-space texts
- whether to indent the first word of new paragraphs
- whether to indent lists, such as this one, and start each item with a capital or small letter
- whether to place headings in the centre of a line or 'flush left' (up against the left margin)
- what typeface to use
- how to write out references to further reading material (see BIBLIOGRAPHIES AND REFERENCES)
- how to signpost footnotes: with an asterisk (*) or a superscript number ([4]) (see BIBLIOGRAPHIES AND REFERENCES)
- how many lines to have on a page of A4. What is the maximum number of characters per line? One useful guide is to have no more than 60 characters per line, which includes letters *and* the spacing between words. Many more than 60 makes for difficult reading.
- whether to 'justify' (even up) the right-hand side of a

text, or leave it 'ragged'? (The latter is easier to read, although it may not look as neat.)

- how to style quotations – whether to put quotation marks around them, or indent them with an empty line above and below to mark them out from the main text.

Many organisations do not have such an explicit house style, so you may have to make your own up. But one thing is important: once you've decided what you'll do, don't vary it within a text. Strive for CONSISTENCY. It is another form of SIGNPOSTING for readers. If you change in mid-stream you may confuse readers.

QUOTE/UNQUOTE

"*If men would only say what they have to say in plain terms, how much more eloquent they would be.*"

Samuel Coleridge (1772–1834)

ILLUSTRATIONS These are a powerful way of communicating with readers. We tend to remember better what we see than what we hear. Visual images have a way of sticking in the mind whereas words often disappear.

'Illustrations' might include photos, drawings, or pictures; diagrams and architectural drawings; or indeed any other visual representation of what is described verbally in the text. For more on this subject, see VISUAL MATERIAL.

IN RESPECT OF... 'In respect of' is a cover-up for laziness, because it is in fact a way of avoiding the decision of which preposition you should really be using: should it be 'for', 'of', 'with' – or some other equally simple short word?

INSTRUCTIONS Instructions are documents that list actions or behaviours that other people have to follow, step by step. If you have to write out instructions for someone you need to place yourself in that person's shoes and ask the questions he or she is likely to have. The assumption behind producing instructions is that they are for people facing a task, or action, for the first time. Instructions may also be reminders for others where a process is long and complicated, or where mistakes can result in major problems.

Some instructions will therefore be short and straightforward, such as those for a fire alarm: these may need no more than a short, clear message about what to do, where to get out of the building, and where to assemble. But other instructions can be considerably more complex.

Instructions are normally step-by-step 'dos and don'ts' in some procedure. So, when writing instructions you need to apply a step-by-step questioning and logic. To someone familiar with a process such minutiae may seem irrelevant or oversimplistic, even childish. This is why it is often useful to have a person relatively new to the task or process to write the instructions. They will still remember the questions, points of indecision, and confusion that arose in their mind when first faced with the task.

What instructions often miss out, yet is helpful to someone new, is to say what *not* to do. It also helps sometimes to list things that may occur but can be ignored. If you are creating a set of instructions containing these last two points you will need to distinguish them from the precise steps that do need to be followed. You might, for instance, place such a text in a different typeface, or put an asterisk in the text, and note these points at the bottom of a page.

INTRODUCTIONS

An introduction, as the name implies, presents to readers a quick statement of what the document that follows is about and aims to do. It's rather like introducing two people to each other: you give an outline or sketch – you don't usually go into too much detail.

An introduction may be part of structured documents such as REPORTS, with a straightforward heading 'Introduction'; or it may simply be the first two or three sentences of a document, and not need any heading. Whichever it is, it will say something briefly about what the document hopes to achieve, or what the writer hopes to convey, or hopes the reader will get – or do. If the introduction precedes a long document it also needs to state briefly how the rest of the document is organised. (See FRONTLOADING.)

An introduction for, say, a longer report, might explain:

- what the document/text is about: the issue, problem, challenge, opportunity, need
- its intention: what it hopes to achieve
- how it arose
- the scope – what is covered
- how the material is organised.

Obviously, introductions will vary depending on the document. If you are writing a letter you may have no need of an introduction other than an opening sentence. (See BEGINNINGS; LETTERS.)

In other instances an introduction may give some background to why the particular document is being written in the first place. If going into such background results in the introduction being several pages long it is better to separate the two and have a heading 'Background'. An introduction should not be too long, for it is simply a text that introduces something more substantial. And remember: the introduction does *not* contain conclusions or recommendations.

INVESTIGATIONS

An investigation is a process of digging out facts, ideas, possibilities. It may be about something in the past or about future potential.

When writing up the results of an investigation (as opposed to proposing that one be set up – see PROPOSALS) you need, as with any written document, to begin with what you mean to investigate, and what prompted you to do so. Was it a past occurrence, or is it some work or activity for the future?

You then need to say what your findings are. If you've been asked to find some solutions, move on to that. A simple outline would be:

1. Issue.
2. Findings.
3. Solution/Recommendation.

Whether you give your solution and/or recommendation before your findings is a matter of choice, but it may also depend on whom your investigation is aimed at. A senior person may be primarily interested in your solution and recommendation. Someone involved in day-to-day activities affected by your findings may want the details, followed by what you judge to be the next step.

If you are investigating several options for some future undertaking you will have a choice of how to write up your findings. After stating the issue (as above) you may then:

- list each option
- give your findings for each
- state the advantages or disadvantages of each
- draw your conclusions
- lastly give your recommendations, along with any caveats about what might be gained or lost by not following certain options.

The important point is to be clear about what you have been asked to do: simply investigate ie stay in 'red' or assess and recommend ways forward ie move into 'blue' and 'green'. (See COLOURS OF WRITING.)

IT, THIS, THAT

The words 'it', 'this', and 'that' can create problems for readers. They often appear at the beginning of sentences and refer to something in a previous sentence (though not necessarily the one immediately preceding). As the writer *you* will know what you are referring to when you write 'it', 'this', or 'that' because you know what your thought processes have been! But make sure these are clear to your readers. Often a train of thought will take a writer temporarily off at a tangent. He or she then returns to the main theme, and begins the next sentence with 'It', 'This', or 'That', which may now refer to something two sentences away. A reader, however, without this insight, may not be quite so sure what 'It', 'This', or 'That' refer to in fact. So just double-check that you are not being ambiguous.

ITEMISING GRAMMATICALLY

When you are writing any document that contains itemised elements or lists you need to make sure that the grammar is correct. So when you write a statement followed by an itemisation (often in the form of one or two sentences per item) every separate item must 'read on' from the initial statement. For example, if you are planning a list of the behaviours required of a manager, it might look (incorrectly) like this:

A manager:

- needs to respond to staff needs
- to listen
- to delegate (etc).

What is wrong here is that the itemised elements do not 'read on' from the opening statement. To do so, the above text should be rewritten in the following way:

A manager needs to:

- respond to staff needs
- listen
- delegate (etc).

You need to go back to the general statement that introduces the list and make sure each one forms a grammatical sentence or phrase. (For two more examples of how this is done, turn to HOUSE STYLE and BIBLIOGRAPHIES AND REFERENCES.)

QUOTE/UNQUOTE

“*Words are . . . the only currency in which we can exchange thought, even with ourselves. Does it not follow, then, that the more accurately we use words, the closer definition we shall give to our thoughts?*”

Sir Arthur Quiller Couch (1863–1944)

JARGON

Jargon is defined as a common language that a group of professionals, specialists, or other people within the same type of work (or even just working for the same organisation) use as a shorthand to convey their meaning. As such, jargon can be very useful.

Where it is less useful, however, is when it is used to communicate with people who are not initiated into it. This applies not only to words but also abbreviations and what they stand for.

If you are writing documents for people not involved in your daily work you may have to find ways of avoiding jargon and explain your meaning in more colloquial English terms! You need to judge your readership.

JOB APPLICATIONS

Writing job applications is something all of us have done, or will do, at some stage of our lives. Hand in hand with these applications go CURRICULUM VITAE. A job application may thus be a combination of the curriculum vitae or c.v. and an accompanying letter which simply says that you are sending a c.v. However, in other instances a job application is a letter with a distinct purpose.

Such a letter may arise out of an advertisement, or you

may be writing 'cold' to make yourself known to someone. If you are responding to an advertisement you need to read it carefully to see what it is really asking for. You then need to explain why the advertisement has attracted your attention. Is it the organisation and what it produces, or where it is located? Or is it specifically the job? Is that job similar to the one you are currently doing or a development in a direction you want to go? Do you feel you have sufficient background and knowledge to tackle it? And what, in your past, leads you to make this assertion? What have you done to illustrate this?

When describing what you have done apply the words that appear in the advertisement and link them to your skills and achievements. Don't simply make a list of your job titles and roles; instead describe your responsibilities, tasks achieved, and successes. Say what you have learnt ie move from 'red' to 'blue' and 'green'. (See COLOURS OF WRITING.)

By doing so you will come across as a person with views and ideas and not simply as a collection of past jobs! If you are then invited to go for an interview remember to do your homework about the new job. Learn as much as possible; and what you can't find out turn into intelligent questions at the interview.

KNITTING TOGETHER

Knitting ideas and thoughts together in a seamless fashion is the mark of good writing. Making sure that the text flows, that the arguments follow one another smoothly, that your sentences are linked in such a way that your reader can follow the train of thought – these all make for what one manager called 'transparent' reading. Your reader isn't pulled up by awkward links. Here are just a few examples of words and phrases that knit a text together:

however	*on the other hand*	*by contrast*	*moreover*
thus	*in other words*	*so*	

Don't, however, confuse these with FLAGWAVERS – phrases that can usually be deleted without losing the thread of the text (or dropping a stitch – to continue the knitting metaphor!).

A text that is well-designed and knitted together may also be one in which you cast off a few stitches. Too many facts and figures (see KNOWLEDGE) may detract from a well-structured and -argued text. (See FACTS AND FIGURES.)

KNOWING ALL YOU CAN

When you write anything, you need to know all that you possibly can about:

- who is going to read it
- why you are writing
- what the content needs to be, in terms of detail, angle, emphasis, and depth of specialised knowledge
- where and when your material will be read.

All these things will give you clues how to present the material. (See READERS – WHO ARE THEY?; SIX Ws; THINK.)

KNOWLEDGE

Knowledge – the content or 'What' (see SIX Ws) of your document – refers to the issues, facts and figures you will be giving or commenting on in your letter, memo, or report. If your knowledge is weak your writing will be also!

Knowing what you are writing about – having a good grasp and clear understanding of the issues – is crucial, no matter whether your document is a letter to a client, a response to a complaint, a report on an event, or whatever. An ill-informed text that gives the wrong facts here or makes false claims there will make the reader distrust the entire document. It smacks of unreliability. Where will the other mistakes and falsehoods be?

So whenever you are using facts and figures always, but always, double-check them. Don't rely only on one source for your facts, unless you have complete confidence in it. Similarly with figures: check them in more than one source if you have any doubts.

When you're stating facts, be precise. 'Most cases of *x* showed that . . .' may not be precise enough. What is the actual number or the proportion of the whole? Similarly such phrases as 'it seems as though . . .' are vague and let the reader know that you aren't too sure. This may be appropriate, but if you can say something more definite such as '*a* is . . .', '*b* is not . . .' then you will appear surer of yourself and your text will be more helpful to your reader.

Where possible, also, don't generalise, unless you are sure that your generalisation is accurate. Statements such as 'all employees feel that . . .' or 'all our goods leave the factory gates in excellent condition' are patently untrue! In the first instance such 'feeling' could not be verified short of interviewing all of those employees; while in the second instance it is truer to say that 'everything is done to try to ensure all goods leave the factory gate in excellent condition'.

If you're not sure of facts in a case you're writing about ask someone reliable or go to other written documents. If you then find discrepant facts or figures try to check which is correct (if there is in fact a correct one – there may be different interpretations or different ways of gathering the figures). If you can't verify the figures, or have different versions of a story, let your reader know. You may then be asked to say which version you think is the most reliable and the one to accept.

Remember though that in many instances you will have been asked to write a document – be it a report or letter – precisely because you do have access to facts and figures, or because you are in fact the 'expert' on that particular subject. This may give you confidence when you sit down and wonder why you have been asked to write a particular piece: your readers may know considerably less about the subject than you. On the other hand this does give you the responsibility to supply readers with unbiased and factual material. And don't forget: you'll be cited as the source in subsequent comments, discussions, or disagreements.

L

LAYOUT All documents – long or short – need to be laid out well. This is what gives them a professional appearance and makes them easy to read. As readers, we pick out such documents in preference to ones that look untidy.

One reason for the appearance being so important is that these days we are surrounded by well-produced visual material in magazines, books, and brochures. We therefore expect other texts and documents to be equally pleasing and attractive to the eye. Good layout begins with the cover of the document; it includes the typeface, how the title is laid out, the colours used, and the general 'feel' and appearance.

When a reader turns to the inside, each page needs to attract, or at least appear easy to read or dip into. In contemporary design much of this attractiveness resides in the tasteful arrangement of white space on a page. Space makes a page look more inviting.

We also look for variety in page design. This can be achieved through the use of illustrations or an interesting – and at the same time helpful – choice of typography. The way that the material is laid out (eg in one or two columns, with bullet points or indenting to highlight material and so on) further increases variety.

An inviting page may also be created simply by having several paragraphs on it. How many of you have looked at a page which consists of text, all in a one-paragraph block, and turned over to the next page in search of something more appealing? Using BULLET POINTS creates a visual highlight, as do HEADINGS.

Consistent page-length in a document is also important for creating a professional visual impact, as is consistency of the typefaces and sizes of headings. Many documents justify (even up) the right-hand side of the text to make it look neat, though in fact it is easier to read a text which is 'ragged right'.

Check your layout for its overall appearance on a printed page, not on a screen. You will see – and be able to judge – the final effect much better. (See EDITING.)

Because good layout is a matter of having a good eye and creating pleasing proportions it is worth talking to a book designer for some guidelines on longer and more complicated documents.

LENGTH

It is obviously not possible to generalise about how long any one document should be. But it is worth remembering that increasingly we all have too much to read and digest. Desks are piled high with material that we all plan to read – when we have the time.

In other words if we can produce shorter documents they are more likely to be read, simply because they will attract a reader more than heavier-looking tomes!

Obviously length depends on purpose. If the purpose is for instance to document a process the text may be long if the process is complicated. Some documents are by their nature long eg scientific reports on work done, or detailed plans for work to be carried out. This is why we produce SUMMARIES for readers who don't want, and don't need, to know the details; or ABSTRACTS with key words, for libraries to record.

Remember however that each reader has some in-built measure of when he or she has read enough on a given subject, has found out enough about it, and can't assimilate any more. We trade information against our own time and interest. A child who was set a book to read over a holiday period and then comment on it wrote the following; 'This book about horses told me more than I wanted to, or was interested in knowing, about horses.' Adults take the same approach.

If a document is turning out to be long ask yourself: 'Do I really need to be writing all of this? Is it relevant? Does my reader really need to know this? Have I explained things in too much detail? Or am I being verbose?'

One way of shortening documents is to put in an appendix some material that you judge not to be vital, but possibly of some interest, to the piece you are writing. (See STORY . . . OR JOURNEY.)

LETTERS

Letters come in different shapes and sizes depending on their purpose, whom they are being written for, and whether they are in response to a previous letter or are the beginning of a correspondence. How to begin and end them seems to be a problem for many writers. They find they have a limited repertoire of standard phrases, and feel unhappy with most of them.

BEGINNINGS

We have a few stock phrases that get rolled out when we have to begin a letter (again, different ones depending on the nature of the letter). Here are just two: 'I am in receipt of your letter of . . . inst.' and 'Further to . . .'. Both sound formal and unfriendly, and not at all like two people talking to each other. Why not try a more reader-friendly, conversational beginning? How about: 'I received your letter of . . . and am responding to the question you raised'; or 'In response to your letter of . . . I would like to give you the following . . .'.

In other words, think what you might *say* to the person receiving the letter. Try out various phrases that seem natural and yet sufficiently formal (or informal).

We often feel we have to put in some polite padding when we begin letters. It is however perfectly possible, and not necessarily abrupt, to go straight to the point. Take a look at 'Letters to the Editor' in various newspapers. They may give you some ideas on how to begin letters by FRONTLOADING them.

FRONTLOADING

Let me use a real-life example of frontloading to illustrate how this can be applied. A friend who had bought a new stove for her kitchen only to find it didn't work began a long letter to the manufacturers describing what had gone wrong and why she was dissatisfied. Only at the end did she say that she wanted her money back. Then, on reflection, she decided that the whole reason she was writing the letter – ie the outcome she wanted – was of course precisely to get her money back. That was the crucial 'why', and not the complaints. So she moved that final sentence to the top of the letter: she frontloaded it.

ENDINGS

What about endings? They often sound insincere and meaningless – for instance: 'In anticipation of your response . . .'; or 'Looking for an early consideration . . .'. Alternatives to these could be: 'I am interested in hearing your views on . .

.'; 'I hope you can let us have a reply by . . .'; or 'I look forward to your thoughts on . . .'.

In other words, try saying what you really want to convey, and then write it. The reader is also a person; sometimes we tend to forget that!

If you can't think of good beginnings and endings, ask colleagues what they do. You'll find a variety of ways of beginning and ending letters, some of which will feel comfortable, and others that won't.

THE 'BODY' OF THE LETTER

As for the 'body' of the letter, it will obviously vary, depending on the reason for writing and on whether you are responding to someone else's letter or writing 'cold'. If you are responding it is a good idea to mark off the points in the letter that you want to comment on, and to do so one at a time. If there are many points, numbering each one may help both you and the reader.

Otherwise use your own sense of logic. Ask yourself: 'What would I want to hear? How would I want the letter structured and written? What would create a good impression on me?'

LOGIC AND LINKING

Whenever we read something attentively our mind becomes engaged and we begin to ask ourselves questions, to anticipate what the writer will touch on next, and in the process we create our own logical thought processes. A document must have a logic and order that it follows; every sentence and every paragraph has to be linked to what comes before and what follows it.

There are two aspects to creating a logical and well-ordered document: one is the overall STRUCTURE; the other is the logic within each thought process, and the development of each idea.

As we write we don't always automatically write logically; we don't make all the links that a reader needs. Our brain often jumps around, goes off at tangents, sees new possibilities. It's important to write these down as they come to mind and then to put them in sequence. This is best done by looking at what you have written – preferably on paper rather than on screen – and then beginning to play around and move texts to their most logical place.

FLOW CHARTS

You may find that drawing a flow chart helps. You put down the step-by-step thinking, the logical sequencing, and then draw arrows to denote movement. Simply seeing what you're creating spread out before you may highlight gaps or illogicalities. Alternatively, it may point up potential connections you've not made before.

This stage – that of ordering your text into a linked, logical sequence – is in a sense a first step in the EDITING process, and may be done when the whole document is finished or when you finish a section or feel you have put down as much as you can on a given issue.

If as a writer you can anticipate some of the questions a reader will ask, and then create headings with those questions incorporated, it will give the reader confidence in the material. It gives energy and development to the text.

PLUGGING THE GAPS

A common problem is however that many writers, familiar

with their subject and engrossed in the writing, make large leaps of thought and assume a reader can follow them. They forget, or are not aware that they need to include, the smaller steps in their thought processes that led to the larger jumps. Such writers need to pace their thinking and writing for their readers.

To help you order your text in smaller steps – be it between sentences or paragraphs – try drawing a flow chart of your thoughts again. How large is the gap or how straight is the line between sentences and paragraphs? Do your thoughts follow step by step or have you jumped across a vast abyss and lost your reader? Are the links smooth or abrupt?

LONG-WINDEDNESS

Long-windedness means using unnecessarily long phrases. Here are a few examples, with their shorter version beside them. Where you can avoid being long-winded, do so!

It was noted that if	–	*if*
It is obvious that	–	*obviously*
It has a tendency to	–	*it tends*
Take into consideration	–	*consider*
For the reason that	–	*because*
In connection with	–	*when, about*
A certain amount of	–	*some*
At the present time	–	*now*
In spite of the fact that	–	*although*
In the majority of instances	–	*usually*

Owing to the fact that	–	*since, because*
A greater length of time	–	*longer*
Afford an opportunity to	–	*allow*
All found to be in agreement	–	*agreed*
During the time that	–	*while*
At that point in time	–	*then*
Have been shown to be	–	*are*
Inasmuch as	–	*because*
Not infrequently	–	*often*
In the vicinity of	–	*near*
In this day and age	–	*now*
Bring to a conclusion	–	*finish, end*

MEANING IS IN PEOPLE

'Meaning is in people, not words.' I don't know who said that, but it is certainly true. Words are symbols; they are the nearest we can get to communicating with others (apart from body language, touch, music, or art). They are therefore bound to contain 'room for error'.

For instance if you and I talk about a table I cannot be sure that even with so tangible an object that we are seeing the same thing. I can only assume that we are. Or take colours: do we see the same red or blue?

Consider what happens when we use words that don't have some tangible reality or instantly create pictures (like 'table' or a colour). If simple terms like 'I'll help you' or 'let's go for a walk' can create ambiguity (does 'help' mean 'I'll do it for you', or 'I'll give you some ideas', or 'I'll work on part of the issue'? Does 'a walk' mean a stroll, a fast pace, or a day's hike?) then what hope is there for conveying more complex meanings?

The trouble usually starts when we use abstract words. An extract from Lewis Carroll's *Through the Looking-Glass* illustrates this point well! Humpty Dumpty and Alice are discussing birthdays; Humpty Dumpty works out that, in a year,

> '. . . there are three hundred and sixty-four days when you might get un-birthday presents – '

'Certainly,' said Alice.

'And only *one* for birthday presents, you know. There's glory for you!'

'I don't know what you mean by "glory",' Alice said.

Humpty Dumpty smiled contemptuously. 'Of course you don't – till I tell you. I meant "there's a nice knock-down argument for you!" '

'But "glory" doesn't mean "a nice knock-down argument," ' Alice objected.

'When *I* use a word,' Humpty Dumpty said, in a rather scornful tone, 'it means just what I choose it to mean – neither more nor less.'

What we need is simply to be aware of this potential ambiguity with abstract words – for we are not about to stop using them. When we do use such words we can often, by providing a specific example of what we mean, give our readers a sense of direction if there is a chance that they might otherwise not fully grasp our meaning. (See ABSTRACT WORDS.)

MEMOS

Memos are written for many purposes (as of course are all documents) and no single format will do for all memos. But essentially they fall into two categories: action and information. Action memos are focused on something that will be *done* as a result of the memo; information ones do simply what their name implies – give information.

ACTION MEMOS

There is one quite easy format to remember that fits many everyday action memos:

O – state the **outcome** you are seeking
P – state the **prompt**: the problem or the possibility
S – state the **solution**.

'Outcome' refers to what results you hope to achieve as a result of the memo: what you want others to do, what you hope will happen, and so on. The 'prompt' could be an existing problem or issue; maybe an idea; a possibility; or an event/action that you or others are hoping will take place. The 'solution' may include the activities you are proposing, what you want others to do, and so on.

The heading of such a memo also needs to be punchy and active (ie not a 'deadhead' – see HEADINGS). So get a verb into it! Don't have just 'Holiday Arrangements' but something that says what it is about holiday arrangements that needs to be looked at. Is the memo for instance, about arranging a timetable for them, or is it to do with the office being closed on certain holidays?

If you are going to follow up something you've mentioned in the memo, furthermore, say at the end that that is what you will do – especially when you are keen to have some follow-up from those to whom you are sending the memo. Signing off by saying 'Do not hesitate to contact me if . . .' (a clichéd ending!) means leaving this responsibility with others, which may not be appropriate. If it's your responsibility, say *you* will contact *them*!

INFORMATION MEMO

A simple structure for an information memo is:

- issue
- information/insight/idea
- assessment/evaluation (if requested).

You may for instance have been asked to investigate an issue. Your reason for writing the memo is thus to provide the relevant information or data, and also your views and opinions if your reader has requested them (see also INVESTIGATIONS). As with the action memo, make sure your 'heading' tells the reader what the memo is about. And if your memo is in response to questions you have been asked to look into refer back to them. Don't expect your reader to have instant recall of what he or she may have asked you to do a few weeks, or even a few days, ago.

Alternatively someone may have asked you to comment on and perhaps recommend some activity that you have experienced eg a training course. You need to ask yourself: what is my main message? Is it just to describe the course or to say what I think or recommend? If the latter, begin with that, and then describe the course.

If neither of these memo formats fits the memo you've been asked to write you will have to work out your own structure. But these two examples may help you to focus more clearly.

MIND-DUMPING

Mind-dumping describes what we often do when beginning to write: simply throw words down on paper or onto a screen in any order. Mind-dumping serves several very useful purposes:

- ✦ It begins to get ideas out of the mind and onto a visible space, to be seen and thought about.
- ✦ It empties the mind, freeing it up to start thinking about the next issues.
- ✦ It simply starts us *writing*, which can release us when we're stuck.
- ✦ It can create the basic pieces of our OUTLINE or structure just by beginning to show us what information we have in our mind and how it can begin to be organised. In doing so it also pinpoints gaps in our thinking or knowledge.

- It produces the material that, subsequently, we can order into a logical, coherent whole. Even if we start with an outline in mind we may find ourselves – as do many writers – writing neither coherently nor logically. Mind-dumping offers a way out of this.

MIND-MAPS

A mind-map, or spider diagram as it is also called, is a diagrammatic way of creating a 'list', or developing an idea. (See Figure 2.) Mind-maps were developed to make use of the right hemisphere, or side, of our brains: those parts that deal with connections, visual material, imagination, and colour. The left hemisphere of the brain deals by contrast with listing, sequencing, numbers, and linear progression.

A number of famous scientists – who (as scientists) would be categorised as left-hemisphere dominant – claim that, ironically, it was the ability to use the right, creative side of their brain that helped them towards their major discoveries, and not solely the left side. Prominent among those who have made this claim were Albert Einstein and Friedrich Kekulé von Stradonitz.*

Mind-maps allow you to draw connections and include elements that simply may not come to mind if a sequential listing is used. They are thus a useful tool when planning a project. But what is their value when writing a letter or report?

If you know there are many things you want to say, but are not quite sure how to – what to link with what, or which order to place things in – then begin with a mind-map. Having all the points laid out before you helps you to see connections and interesting cross-references. Of course this

* *This is not the place to expand on this subject but* Use Your Mind *by Tony Buzan is an excellent introduction.*

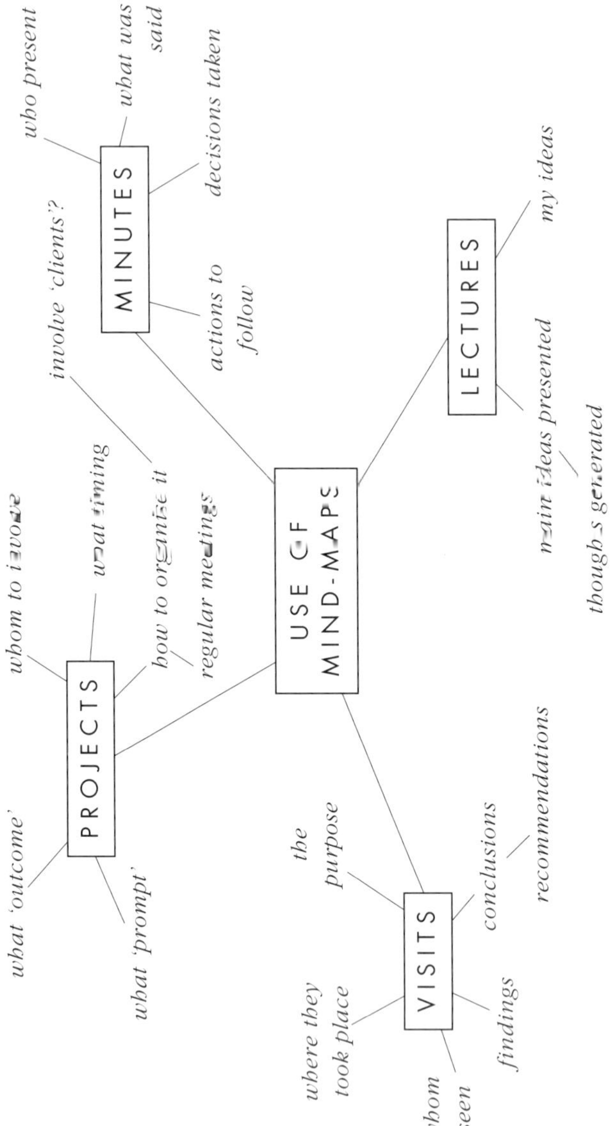

Figure 2 Mind-Maps

diagrammatic form needs eventually to be translated into a verbal, sequential one, which is when the left side of the brain comes into its own. To create our best ideas – and writing – we need both sides to be fully used.

From a mind-map you can go on to create an outline structure. By simply looking at what you've written on it you begin to see what, logically, needs to be written about first, and what then follows. Thus you begin to form a structure.

The mind-map also comes to your help when you need to think about headings and create signposts for your readers. The words or 'items' listed within it and along its branches show you a number of subject areas, and hence potential headings. As you go along the branches you also begin to realise what levels you need to allocate to the various HEADINGS.

A mind-map may also be useful at the beginning of a project that you are organising with a view to producing a report. You can use it for instance to plan an investigation, to make sure you have covered every angle and possibility. Write down the issue in the 'centre' and then put down whatever comes to mind in connection with it. In this sense a mind-map is simply a brainstorm on paper.

MINUTES

Minutes are the notes that record what is said and agreed at a meeting. Their intention is to remind people, and to capture ideas.

It is difficult to know how detailed to make such minutes. Obviously recording verbatim what everyone said is not needed. What the minute-taker needs to do, however, is to capture the essence of what is said. Sometimes this merely means capturing in summarised form what was decided, and not necessarily each of the arguments put forward before the particular decision was taken. On the other hand, putting in the differing viewpoints and contributions expressed means that the minutes more accurately record what did take place, rather than simply the outcomes.

The person who takes the minutes (often the one designated secretary to the meeting, although the role of minute-taker may be a rotating one that everyone takes on for a meeting) doesn't need any particular writing skills but does need to be a good listener. The minutes are then written up under the various points and headings listed in the AGENDA. The problem is that if they are too short they will give little for readers to hold onto (particularly those who weren't present); but if too verbose they simply become tiresome to read.

When written up over a series of meetings these minutes form a convenient overview of the work of a particular group of people.

N

NEVER ONE WAY

There is never just one way of expressing something. Your version, provided it is grammatically correct and coherent, is as good as anyone else's. Others may express themselves more elegantly and use a wider range of words, so there will always be differences. After all, each of us speaks differently. Why shouldn't we write differently too?

This point should be borne in mind by anyone editing another person's text. Just because an editor would prefer to express something in their own way doesn't give them the right arbitrarily to change someone else's words. Yes, by all means change what isn't clear or grammatical. But editors shouldn't simply alter words in order to leave their mark on a text. That is not the purpose of editing.

Even before your piece is edited by someone else you, the writer, can replace existing sentences and ways of expressing an idea: there is no phrase or sentence that cannot be rewritten. Words are there to be placed in different relationships with one another, to be played with to see which sounds best, or is the cleverest.

It is worth emphasising this point. Many writers, unhappy with their first attempts, merely tinker with those existing sentences and phrases, apparently afraid to abandon what they've already written and start anew. Take for example the following three ways of saying the same thing:

1 'If you are expected to produce documents that are well structured and coherently written, the opportunity and environment need to be provided.' (This is clumsily phrased.)

2 'If you are expected to produce documents that are well structured and coherently written you need to be given the opportunity and environment in which to do so.' (Only slightly better; still needs rewording.)

3 'If your manager expects you to write documents that are well structured and coherently written, he/she needs to give you the time and space in which to achieve that.' (Better, because it identifies what 'opportunity' and 'environment' might mean; but could still be improved.)

NEWSLETTERS

Newsletters are a newspaper and a magazine in miniature, rolled into one, and a vehicle for both serious and chatty items. Which it is to be, or whether a combination of both, is for an editor and those for whom the newsletter is being produced to decide. Newsletters thus provide an opportunity for people to write in either a formal or conversational STYLE.

A newsletter should have a professional look if it is to be read with pleasure and ease. It is worth asking a designer to provide a layout to suit its purpose and be acceptable to its READERS. A newsletter intended to be literally 'newsy' would probably have a layout resembling those in newspapers or magazines ie two or three (or more) columns per page, items in 'boxes', and highlighted texts. If the intention is to produce a more serious publication the newsletter may simply have one column of text on every page and thus look more like a book than a newspaper.

As with any written document the main things to be clear

about are who the readers will be and what their interests are. Why would they want to read the newsletter? The answer to these questions will give a focus for what goes into the publication.

The role of a newsletter editor is to decide who will write the material and how much of the contributors' copy he or she as editor will change. Does the newsletter in question need to have an overall, consistent writing style? Any such style will, of course, follow other editorial rules on consistency. (See CONSISTENCY; EDITING.)

NUMBERING

Always number the pages of any document. It makes reference easier should you need to discuss the text with someone else later. It also helps when, inadvertently, the document is dropped on the floor and the pages get scattered, or it is faxed through somewhere in the wrong order.

There are other things that you might also consider numbering: diagrams, ilustrations, and tables in any text have to be numbered sequentially, and cross-references given in the text. Numbering headings or items within sections may also be helpful, particularly in a longer or more complex document. But beware of excessive numbering, for example '1.1.1' to refer to a sub-heading in point 1 of chapter 1.

OHP TRANSPARENCIES

OHP (overhead projector) transparencies serve two purposes. They are an *aide-mémoire* for the person using them – the presenter or trainer; they also help an audience to see what they are hearing, and hence memorise it better. It is claimed that we remember 30 per cent of what we see 48 hours after seeing it, but only 10 per cent of what we hear.

The transparency needs to be laid out in a clear way – with a heading at the top. For a transparency to work effectively it should not have too many words on it.

If the purpose is to use the transparency to talk from (as most trainers and presenters do) it may be helpful to write down key words or phrases, with sufficient spacing between each for readers to glance down them with ease. The typeface needs to be large, and the text written in capital letters. It may also help to number the items, or place a bullet point before each one (or dashes if a word processor doesn't have bullet points on it!). Colour on transparencies to highlight different elements in their text greatly improves their appearance.

Transparencies are useful for conveying ideas or relationships by backing up the words used with drawings, cartoons, diagrams, mind-maps, or simply by creating connections. If a speaker is referring to numbers and figures, showing them on transparencies is probably the only way to help an audience understand and remember them.

A transparency with some general key words can be used to introduce a topic. The entire content of a talk or workshop can then be conveyed on several transparencies. Finally, a transparency can sum up what has been said, again by using key words. Well-thought-out and laid-out transparencies can then be photocopied and given to the audience or workshop participants. (See TRAINING MATERIALS.)

OUTCOMES AND ACHIEVEMENTS

These may seem strange words to include in a book on writing. They are, however, crucial.

You are writing because you want something to happen, something to be achieved, as a result of your text being read. You want some action taken, some ideas pursued, you want someone to understand a process, or to be satisfied with answers to questions, and so on. In other words, you expect a result: an outcome. Keeping the outcome firmly in your head helps you to focus on whether what you are writing leads to that outcome, or whether you are digressing (see Figure 3).

Being clear about this will mean that your introductory sentences or paragraphs are more focused and coherent. You'll be able to tell your readers immediately why you're writing (see FRONTLOADING). By stating the outcome early you avoid leaving your reader to hunt around to discover why you've sent him or her the document, and why they should read it. What follows here is a 'focus document' to help you achieve this goal.

FOCUS DOCUMENT

These points will help you to be clear why you're sending someone a particular document.

Figure 3
Step Diagram

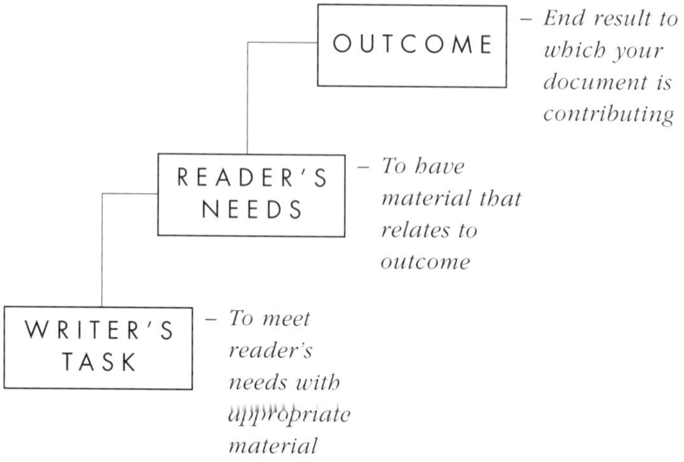

1. This document is about . . .
2. Its aim is to (describe, suggest) . . . so that . . . (*x* will take place, *y* will be avoided)
3. I am sending it to you because . . .
4. What I hope you will be able to do after reading it is . . .

OUTLINE

An outline is vital for any document. I prefer to use this word in the early days of planning a document rather than STRUCTURE. Structure has something too pre-ordained about it. An outline – like an architect's first drawing – gives a text its first, loose shape. It can be changed and developed; it can be altered and redrawn. What begins life as a many-storeyed tower may become a single-storey building.

The outline is therefore just the initial shape you give to

a document – any document. It may emerge as you begin to write and let your ideas start to flow. It may emerge from the GIST of what you want to say – a really short version, maybe anything from a dozen or so sentences to three or four paragraphs – that can then be built on to create a longer document. Or it may emerge if you create a MIND-MAP or some other diagrammatic form such as a flow chart.

When creating this outline you don't need to start with the foundations (the beginning) and work through to the roof (the conclusions and recommendations). All the bits fall into shape eventually, so begin with whatever is easiest – be kind to yourself! Working on the easiest bits will give you a sense of achievement. Tackling the more difficult bits is then not such a major problem, and what seemed like an impossibility may fall into place as you go along.

Once you have got your ideas in some shape you can begin to think of the LOGIC and how you can best convey your message. For that you need to be clear what that is. It might be what your research has uncovered; what you want to achieve; what your reader will be able to do after reading your document; or what you want people to do after receiving your memo; and so on. Decide what it is, and that will give you clues about the best structure to use in order to convince your readers. After all, one of the main intentions every writer has is to convince his or her readers that what they are reading is 'the best' for the purpose.

PARAGRAPHS Contrary to what many writers think, a paragraph is not an item of length: it is an item of information or a development of an idea, theme, or argument. A paragraph is a collection of sentences that develop any of these. As you write you may of course find that you are developing a theme or idea at some length, and that your so-called paragraph now fills a whole page. If this happens go back and see where you could, for the reader's benefit, break up the text to start new paragraphs. You'll find the breaks at the point where you begin an alternative development, or offer a different view, or move to some new angle.

As you move on to new topics and issues you must, once more for the reader's benefit, start a new paragraph. Readers need 'space' and time to digest what they have read. This may be only a split-second – merely the time it takes to move the eye from one chunk of text to the next. But it's enough. It's the psychological space that matters. How many of you have looked at a page of writing with only two paragraphs on it or, worse still, just one? And what do you normally do when faced with such a page? Turn over to find a more appealing and inviting one?

Because a paragraph is a unit of connected thoughts, if you want to keep track of what you are saying in it, to make sure you do not wander off into other themes, put a 'temporary' heading above each paragraph to keep you on track and stop you from digressing too much.

Try on average (and this is only a guide, not a rule) to keep paragraphs to no more than 10 lines of text. That will be, on an A4 page, approximately 100 words. And that in turn is around five sentences long.

Remember also that paragraphs need to follow one another logically. If you are changing the subject of a paragraph dramatically from the preceding one, warn your reader. Do so with an introductory phrase such as 'By contrast . . .', or 'There are, however, other points of view . . .', and so on. You need to choose an appropriate phrase. If you don't make this link you may lose your reader, who will be left confused, maybe angry, and certainly wondering about the logic of your thinking processes.

These leaps into the dark often happen when writers don't lead readers through their thought processes; they make assumptions about the readers' ability to follow unstated thoughts. In short, they expect clairvoyance! So every sentence needs to link with the ones that both come before and after it.

In trying to avoid overly long paragraphs don't go in the opposite direction and make them just one sentence long – unless you want the message contained in it to stand out because it is an important point. (See also LOGIC AND LINKING.)

PLAN

(see OUTLINE)

POLYSYLLABIC WORDS

Polysyllabic words (such as the word 'polysyllable' itself, which has five syllables) are difficult to digest. It is not because they are incomprehensible but because the reader expends effort simply reading them. They make for marginally more difficult reading (see FOG INDEX). In many instances we can't, as writers, avoid them; they may be part and parcel of a vocabulary we have to use (often professional jargon), or they might really be the best word in the circumstance.

But be aware there may be simpler, shorter words that express the same thing and are often clearer. Alternatively such words, which are frequently nouns created out of shorter verbs, can be recycled back to their verbal form (see RECYCLING WORDS). To help in the search for words with a similar or identical meaning (synonyms) a DICTIONARY or THESAURUS are a must for those who take their writing seriously. For examples of some polysyllabic words, see CHOOSE THE FAMILIAR WORD.)

POMPOSITY

I use this word with some trepidation,* since much of what I want to highlight here is in common use in many organisations! A pompous text uses language that would rarely, if ever, be heard in conversation. For instance: 'We are in receipt of your letter of . . . inst.' Why not simply say, 'We have received your letter of July . . .'? Why not say, instead of 'Looking for an early consideration . . .', 'Will you please let us know . . .', or some other phrase?

Often these pompous phrases are ones we use without even thinking. They are so common that possibly we don't even notice them as they flow from the pen or appear on the screen. But if we are trying to improve written communication they need to go!

I have tried in this book to avoid such words and phrases, and use instead more direct, everyday, conversational

** Trepidation is, I am aware, a word ending in -tion (see* RECYCLING WORDS*), and has four syllables in it (see* FOG INDEX*). However, having looked in the thesaurus, I found it most nearly conveyed the feeling I wanted to express. The word 'fear' did not fit the bill.*

language. This has meant that I have – I hope – created a document that is informal in STYLE and conveys what I want it to say, without wrapping it up in verbiage.

POSITIVE LANGUAGE

Stating things in a positive, rather than negative, way can have an equally positive impact on your reader. Consider the following examples of positive and negative ways of putting things, and be aware of what each does to you ie do you feel a sense of energy when you hear the positive, or the negative?

'Our sales figures have slumped.'
'We need to improve our falling sales figures.'
'We have no system for . . .'
'We need to create a system for . . .'

Obviously there is nothing to be gained by lying, and this is not the point of being positive. You should merely be aware of what effect a negative statement may have on your reader. Negative feelings often lead to negative energy. So if you want to encourage your reader to go off and do something you are more likely to get that response from a statement that contains some forward-looking words or phrases than from one that leaves the reader literally slumped in his or her chair!

Some years ago Coca-Cola ran an advertisement claiming 'This Cola has no sugar' – which the company thought was a bonus. Yet it resulted in a fall in sales. Market research uncovered the fact that the word 'no' had been subconsciously interpreted as 'Don't drink Cola'. Their next advertisement read, 'This Cola is sugar-free', and sales rose again.

PROOFREADING

Proofreading is the final stage in the writing cycle (see Figure 1). It is your final check that all the corrections included at the EDITING stage have been done and that the whole document looks professional.

To proofread a document you need to read every word carefully – and not just skim through as you might if you were simply reading the document. The only way to ensure you proofread properly is to do so line by line, with a ruler or piece of paper that you move down the page you are checking. In other words, to do a proper proofreading job you need to have a printout of a document, and not do it on screen. Take particular care to read the title and headings – they often get missed at this final stage of checking.

You will also now be able to put in the page numbers on a table of contents, if there is one. This is also the time to double-check that any numbering (eg of tables and figures) is correct and consistent.

Even if you are sending out a short document – maybe one only a page long – do a proofreading job on that, too. Professionalism pays off.

PROPOSALS

Many of us frequently have to write proposals. They may come in the form of asking someone to back up an idea you have, or perhaps to agree to your going on a course; or they may be 'genuine' proposals – to provide a new service, to run a new training course, or maybe to write a book.

While there is no single format for proposals each has to follow a logical train of thought. If you want to convince someone of the sense of your proposal, and persuade them to accept it (presumably the purpose of most proposals!), you need to be clear and logical. Below are a few step-by-step ideas which most proposals would incorporate.

A GENERAL PROPOSAL:

1. A title, and a few lines stating clearly what you are proposing.
2. State how the idea arose and give some background eg say whether someone else proposed it, or whether it is your idea or one you've seen elsewhere, whether there is an obvious need for it etc.
3. State next in what way you think your proposal is needed, is valuable, or will be of benefit; and state who will benefit. Mention also (if it's relevant) what might happen if your proposal is not accepted.
4. It may be useful, again only if it is relevant, to mention whether something similar already exists – or not; if it does, say how your proposal differs.
5. Describe now your proposal in more detail. If you are proposing a new 'product' say how it will differ from those already on offer. If you have tested out some actions or ideas and rejected them, state this also.
6. If you are able, or if it is relevant, give the costs, resources needed, and how you hope to address these.
7. Lastly, express your hope that you have given the reader enough material to help him or her take a decision, but if this is not the case, say you will be happy to provide more.

A TRAINING PROPOSAL:

1. Title: proposal to run . . .
2. An outline (two or three sentences).
3. How it arose: a request, a perceived need, etc.

4 Who would benefit, and in what way.

5 Outline of actual course or programme.

6 Other details about costs, length, frequency, etc.

Make sure any proposal you write is typed out, even if it is short and informal. It shows you are being professional about it. It needs to be laid out clearly and be signposted with headings, bullet points, and clear paragraphs. It you are making several points it may help to number them so that readers can refer to and discuss individual points later on.

PUNCTUATION

Punctuation is the bane of many writers' lives. Where should you put full stops or commas; when should you use a colon or a semi-colon?

Bad punctuation – that is, punctuation used inappropriately – is not only confusing for readers: it can so annoy them that they cease to read a document for its content and instead look for the next mistake. And given the wide availability of various programs on word processors to help with grammar, such sloppiness will annoy even more. It smacks of the writer saying, 'Here are my thoughts; it's up to you, the reader, to make sense of them, not for me to consider you.' Bad punctuation may not only ruin a good piece of work but also change the sense of what has been written. Let me illustrate with just two examples.

- Imagine a telegram (where each letter costs) with the words: 'Kill not coming.' Depending on where you put the full stop, the meaning is completely altered: 'Kill. Not coming' or 'Kill not. Coming.'
- Imagine a sentence such as: 'Truck drivers, whose minds are dull, do not survive long.' With a slight alteration this becomes: 'Truck drivers whose minds are dull do not survive long.' One is insulting, the other defines certain drivers.

Faced with bad punctuation a reader will often begin to pass judgement on the writer's general ability. If a writer can make casual mistakes with punctuation, have they been equally casual with the content? Can they be trusted? Worse: the reader will probably begin to wonder about the section, department, or organisation where the writer works. If they produce sloppy writing they may also produce sloppy services or goods. So, back to the main items of punctuation.

Where do you place full stops and commas? There is one very simple way of gauging that: read the sentence out loud and listen to your voice. It will tell you where to put a comma (where your voice stops briefly) and where to place a full stop (where your voice drops and stops). By doing this you'll also notice that, by and large, we speak in short sentences. They're easier to follow. So use punctuation to say what you want to say simply and clearly. Another clue to where full stops should go in long sentences is where you have placed such words as 'and', 'but', or 'however'.

Commas are also used in lists to separate out items. Their use is strictly to help readers understand. Another place where they are used, therefore, is to separate clauses from main sentences: for instance, 'The supervisor, who had not worked on the night shift before, came in an hour early.'

Do remember, though, that when you reread what you have written and decide you need, say, to add a full stop in order to make the text more readable, you should go back and reread (at least) the sentence preceding the one with the new full stop. You should also read the new sentence that follows, to make sure you still have a complete sentence ie one containing a main verb. Without a verb, a string of words is not a sentence, and hence is ungrammatical.

When do you use colons and semi-colons? A colon (:) is normally used to precede a list, or to state and highlight one item. An example might be this sentence: 'She wanted to make the point: no one would be discriminated against.' You would need a colon in a sentence such as, 'John listed the following items he wanted for the meeting: the minutes of the previous one, the list of members' addresses, the letters of application he had received, and a notepad to write on.'

In that sentence the commas are sufficient to divide off the items in the list. If however each item was described in further detail a semi-colon (;) would make the reading much easier: 'John listed the following items: the minutes of the previous meeting, although he knew they had not been circulated to the members; the list of members' addresses, although he had forgotten to photocopy it; . . .' and so on.

A semi-colon thus has two major uses. One is in lists, as we've seen above. Its other main use is to replace a full stop where there are two thoughts so closely connected that placing a full stop between them thereby creating two sentences, would somehow separate them too much. For instance: 'John went home to Yorkshire; it was the first time he had been back for several years'; or 'They wanted to write the report; they felt sure it would raise the profile of the department.' In both of these instances a full stop could, grammatically, replace the semi-colon.

The apostrophe creates another problem, especially when it is combined with the letter s ('s, s'). Here it is used to show possession eg 'the woman's bank account' or 'the women's bank accounts'. Its other common use is to fill the place of another letter that isn't there (as in 'isn't': the apostrophe replaces the 'o' of 'not'). Similarly we have 'it's' short for 'it is'. What confuses many people, however, is the possessive 'its' ('of it'). For example: 'The company placed its logo above the main doorway.' It is wrong to write: 'The company placed it's logo . . .'

For anyone confused or uncertain about grammar and punctuation, I suggest some simple book or guide to serve as a useful reminder and 'crib' eg G. V. Carey's *Mind the Stop* (London, Penguin Books, 1976).

PURPOSE

(see WHY ARE YOU WRITING?)

QUOTE/UNQUOTE

"*At times [a writer] may indulge himself with a long [sentence], but he will make sure there are no folds in it, no vagueness, no parenthetical interruptions of its view as a whole; when he has done with it, it won't be a sea-serpent with half of its arches under the water; it will be a torchlight procession.*"

Mark Twain (1835–1910)

QUESTIONS IN TEXTS

Posing questions in a text is a good way of showing a reader how your thinking is developing. In this sense questions are a form of SIGNPOSTING. If your piece follows a clear logic your readers may well be asking themselves the same questions that you pose. That is what happens as we read: our mind flags up silent, unspoken questions. So by asking questions you may anticipate the ones your readers have. This will give readers confidence in you. If, on the other hand, you ask questions they haven't thought of, that will also increase their interest.

Another place for questions is in titles or headings. They give readers some indication of what is to follow, a focus, so that they can in turn adjust their own thinking appropriately. They may also signal to readers what information or knowledge to retrieve from the hidden corners of their memory. The result of posing such questions may be, alternatively, to begin turning the cogs in the readers' own minds on the issues raised by those questions. The readers are then more prepared for the text that follows. All of this, of course, occurs instantaneously and subconsciously.

QUOTATIONS

Quotations (also called – improperly – 'quotes') are of course citations of other people's words and are commonly used in many documents. They back up our own material or ideas, or that of others which we are working on or responding to.

If you are quoting a long text by someone else it is helpful to the reader if you separate it from your own words. You can do this by simply arranging the texts on separate lines, and putting the quoted material in inverted commas (''). You might also indent the quoted lines to make them stand out more from the rest of the text. Alternatively you can put them into *italics*, or use a different typesize ie slightly smaller than the one you are using for the rest of the text.

If the quotation is long – more than, say, five lines – and isn't integral to what you are trying to convey then it may make more sense to place it at the end of the document and cross-refer readers to it. (See BIBLIOGRAPHIES AND REFERENCES.)

QUOTE/UNQUOTE

“*A book that furnishes no quotations is . . . no book – it is a plaything.*”

Thomas Love Peacock (1785–1866)

READERS: WHO ARE THEY?

You need to know who your readers are, for without that information you can't write a document that meets their needs and is appropriate for them. It is for them you are writing, not for yourself – something many writers seem to forget! Just consider two simple cases. Would you write the same kind of letter to your grandmother and your lover, your children and your boss?

Whatever you write, you need to make sure that you have catered for your readers' needs and interests, and have taken into account their level of knowledge of the relevant subject. But most importantly you need to be clear why you are writing something for them ie identify what OUTCOMES you and they are looking for. You also need to be sure, if your readers have particular expectations of your document, that you meet them; if they asked you to address certain subjects or issues, that you have done so.

How can you find out who your readers are? You can ask others who have written to them or dealt with them in some other way. Alternatively you can speak to your reader, if there is only one person, and ask what it is they want or need to have from you. If you're responding to a request or letter make sure you fully understand what is wanted. If in any doubt ask for clarification.

Even if you are writing for a number of readers you still

need to get a flavour of who they are: some sort of profile. This is important because if you find they are a widely disparate group you will need to consider seriously whether you can get away with writing one document or whether you ought to produce more than one; maybe one will be enough, but with different sections for different readers and some appendices. Another option may be to cater for different needs by producing different SUMMARIES.

If you have a diverse group of readers, and their level of knowledge is varied, you will also have to adjust the content and language of your text. A lot of technical or highly specialised words may for instance be totally inappropriate.

Ideally, to help yourself and make your task – and your life – easier, try to find out the following about your readers:

- who they are
- what positions they hold
- what level of knowledge they have
- what their particular interest is in your material
- what their reason is for reading it.

This will give you some idea of the type of text you should write, the detail you need to include, the language to use, and the style. (See SIX Ws.)

RECYCLING WORDS

Recycling, as the word implies, means changing something back into a substance or item that it once was, or at least resembled. Thus paper and glass are recycled into different sorts of paper and glass. And so it is with words.

There are many words we currently use – mostly nouns – that have emerged from verbs. In most instances the verbs are shorter, and a great deal punchier, than the long nouns that pepper most written documents. For instance: 'development' comes from 'to develop'; 'connection' comes from 'to connect'.

Other such words – and you will recognise them because they end in -ibility, -ment, and -tion – include:

- possibility. 'There is the possibility that . . .' can be recycled back into 'It is possible that . . .'
- availability. 'The lack of availability of machines posed a problem' recycled back becomes 'No machines were available, which posed a problem.'
- commencement. 'Before the commencement of term, the students . . .' recycled back becomes 'Before term commenced, the students . . .
- clarification. 'We asked for clarification of the terms of the agreement . . .' recycled back becomes 'We asked *X* to clarify the terms of the agreement.'

These are just a few examples. The value in turning them back – recycling them – to the verbs they originally were is that sentences with verbs are punchier, have an element of action in them, and are often more focused.

So when you find yourself using one of these words, stop and think: would the sentence sound better, be more precise, and have more action in it if you were to use the verb and not the noun? (See ENERGY.)

REPORTS

Reports come in various shapes and sizes. They can be two or 200 pages long; they can have a structure imposed on them (eg progress or visit reports) or their structure can be left to the ingenuity of the writer.

Essentially, though, a report is a diamond-shaped

document (see Figure 4). If it is a long document, it will start with a SUMMARY – a short one- or two-page précis of what is in each part of the report itself. Next there will be an INTRODUCTION to the overall report possibly made up of a background section, a main body, conclusions, and lastly recommendations. This is a pretty standard shape for a report.

Figure 4
The diamond

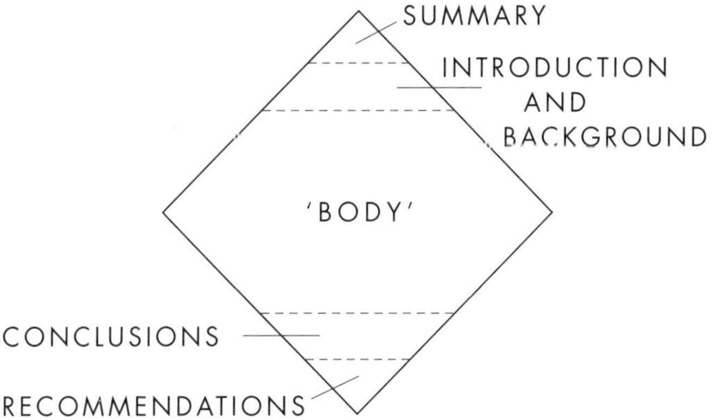

There are variations on this theme, a common one being to have the introduction precede the summary. This is no more than a matter of where to place things but, logically, since a summary contains a summary of the introduction, it should precede it.

Another variation on the theme of a report is where the writer is asked to study a number of options or possibilities and offer arguments as to which should be followed. This will still have a diamond shape, but the headings will vary. (See ARGUMENTS, SUGGESTIONS AND IDEAS.)

As with any other document, a report needs a good title

– one that describes what it is actually about. It may reflect the findings more than the actual information that has been gathered, let alone how it was gathered.

You may find it an interesting exercise to read through some of your reports to see where (indeed, if) you told the reader why the work reported on was undertaken in the first place. This needs to be stated early in the introduction, yet in many instances it is hidden away, often lurking at the end of the third or fourth paragraph! If this happens in your reports you need to FRONTLOAD your document.

Long reports need headings – not only to help the reader through them, but also to keep the writer on track and to ensure that the document flows in a logical fashion. HEADINGS help enormously to maintain this flow.

Most of all you need to write reports in such a way that if you were yourself the reader you would find them logical and convincing. (See LOGIC AND LINKING.)

A problem that people face when working on a long report is that they may not be the only writer. There may be several people contributing to the final document. Unless there is a good briefing, with all writers present, the editor of the final piece will have a daunting job making the report look and feel as though it has been written by one person. Although it may be difficult to disguise different styles of writing there must be some agreement on the overall style, as well as on the layout, use of capitals, abbreviations, and a host of other issues. If the organisation has a HOUSE STYLE the task may not be too difficult. If it doesn't then the editor must establish some common ground rules.

Many people find writing reports very daunting. They get worried by the implications. A report sounds like a really weighty document, and many feel they're not up to it. They feel much happier, however, writing a letter. So if the actual word 'report' produces negative feelings in you, call what you have to write by some other name, and see if that frees you up (eg 'my thoughts/findings on . . .').

If you're still worried by the notion of writing a report write the shortest version you can think of – the GIST. Even if this is only a page long it will contain the main elements that you need to expand on. And as you begin to do so you will probably think of other points to make. And so your report may begin to take shape, in outline. (See ARGUMENTS, SUGGESTIONS, AND IDEAS; INTRODUCTIONS; SUMMARIES.)

REREAD EVERYTHING

Reread what you write – either after trying to convey a complex idea or after a few sentences or paragraphs, and above all when you think you have finished writing. Never send off a text without first rereading it!

Exactly *when* you choose to reread is a matter of personal choice. But a word of warning: don't keep stopping to do so, because that might halt your creative flow!

As you reread you'll spot places where you may have altered the shape of a sentence but forgotten to check the sentence before and after the altered one, to make sure the whole made sense and was grammatical. (See EDITING.)

RHYTHM AND FLOW

The rhythm and flow of a text are what makes it easy, satisfying, and pleasurable to read. There is nothing wrong in trying to give your readers pleasure. There is too much drab and uninspired writing travelling around most organisations at present!

So how do you achieve rhythm in a text? You achieve it by varying the structure and length of sentences. You achieve it by making sure that links between sentences are smooth. You achieve it by making sure the logic of your thinking flows naturally, and doesn't dart around, losing your readers – and often yourself – in the process. And you achieve it by the way words fall into a rhythm. Let me give an example. Elsewhere in this book I wrote the three words 'E-mail, memo, or report'. I could have written 'report, memo, or E-mail', but the second version doesn't trip as easily off the tongue as the first. (Even this paragraph, itself, has a certain rhythm, based on the repetition of 'you achieve'.)

You'll know whether you've achieved a rhythm in your own writing by reading out loud what you have written and listening to the flow. You will hear if sentences end abruptly; you will be able to recognise where, by moving the order of certain words, you literally get a better rhythm (as in the example just given). Writing well is not unlike composing music. (See LOGIC AND LINKING.)

S

SAY IT

Say it. That's the key to improving your writing. If it sounds wrong when spoken, scrap what you've written and start again.

You will find that complicated and convoluted sentences can always be replaced with simpler, spoken sentences. We speak in short SENTENCES. We also speak with relative coherence. There is no reason why a coherently expressed sentence shouldn't appear in writing.

If what you've written is complicated, stilted, and long-winded, stop and ask yourself, 'What am I trying to *say*?' Then write down what you've said. Yes, it will need some editing to remove ungrammatical spoken language (we all occasionally speak ungrammatically, or don't finish our sentences). But at least you will have the gist of something coherent and simple to work on.

SENTENCES

A sentence is a unit of thought. It can be extended and become a development of a thought, but if more than two such developments are kept within one sentence it risks becoming long and complex. Another way to define a sentence – particularly when you're writing one and need to punctuate it correctly – is to think of it as a unit of 'sense': it's defined at the beginning by a capital letter and ends when the sense ends, with a full stop.

If you're unsure about recognising a sentence – as you write it – begin simply, with a short thought, literally stating something plain and straightforward. Place a full stop after that initial thought. Then create a new sentence from the next thought. No matter if these initial sentences have only four or five words in them: once you've put two or three down see whether – and how – they might be linked to form one longer sentence. But better more short sentences than one long one if it is going to become too complex.

Because sentences are the basis on which any document is built you could think of them as the muscles, the energy of your writing. They give a document its life and movement. Like muscles they can be stiff and turgid, or flexible and active. The energy in a sentence, or lack of it, will vary depending on how the VERBS are used, how many subordinate phrases (such as this one) are included – which could make the sentence unwieldy, and the language and vocabulary used.

There are no hard and fast rules about the length of sentences. But, to give you a guide, a sentence that has more than 20 words in it will begin to get complex. Most sentences that are longer can easily be broken down into shorter ones without creating childlike simplicity. On the contrary, they will often add clarity to your text.

Longer sentences often lose the reader – and even the writer! It is easy to lose sight of the main subject of a long sentence and begin to drift off in other directions. Often the result is singular subjects and plural verbs; verbs that lose sight of which tense they should be in; and, most confusing of all for the reader, a complete change of subject matter, which will force them to stop and reread what you have written. That is a bad sign, unless the concept or information you are trying to convey is indeed very complex, and the reader needs to return because they simply didn't grasp what you were getting at the first time round. (Note that this last sentence is very long and, although punctuated quite carefully, could nevertheless have been written differently, with shorter sentences.)

Short sentences are useful if you want to emphasise a point or create a sense of drama. They have an energy that longer sentences don't have. But too many of them becomes irritating and may – particularly if the writer's vocabulary is limited – make the text sound too childlike. Yet there is nothing inherently wrong with four- or five-word sentences.

There are a number of clues that a sentence may become long:

- Sentences that begin with 'Although', 'Because', 'In spite of', and similar phrases will often end up long. You can shorten them by beginning with the second half of the sentence, thus creating the first part of a new sentence (rewritten, of course).
- Some sentences are long because they contain too much padding or begin with FLAGWAVERS. Padding is what we do when we feel a sentence will sound grander or carry more 'weight' simply if it has more words in it.
- Long sentences usually occur where the writer is not sticking to the rule: one thought, one sentence; a new thought, a new sentence. Or they are trying to cram everything about the subject matter of the sentence into one whole. They do this with a string of 'ands' or 'buts', and phrases beginning with 'which' or 'when'.

So when you've written what you think is a sentence, read it out loud. Is it one? Does it make sense? Does the long string of words you've strung together form a sentence? Listen to your voice. If it stops or falters you'll know there's something wrong. Stop and look at the sentence: is the punctuation wrong? Is there no verb in it? Is it simply too long and complicated?

SIGNPOSTING

Signposting is a way of helping the reader through your text. The obvious way to do this is to use HEADINGS that explain what is to follow. In this sense headings can anticipate questions that may be in the reader's mind; or they can provoke questions.

The other way of signposting is to create PARAGRAPHS. They inform the reader that there is a slight change in direction or a change of subject.

A third way of signposting is to use other visual means such as BULLET POINTS to tell the reader there are some important matters to be aware of. Numbering items is another way of achieving the same result.

Less obvious signposting can be achieved by using a visual image to attract the reader's eye, or by using the LAYOUT on a page to draw a reader's attention. (See HIGHLIGHTING TEXT; TABLE OF CONTENTS.)

SITUATION: A SUPERFLUOUS WORD

'We have a crisis situation' is a classic example of using a superfluous word. The sentence 'we have a crisis' is perfectly adequate, and grammatical. Moreover it is actually punchier and conveys the sense of crisis better! 'Situation' adds nothing – is, in fact, meaningless in this context. The *Oxford English Dictionary* has several definitions of the word 'situation': it can mean someone's position in relation to others; it can be a place; or a conjunction of circumstances. So here are three other words that might instantly replace the well-loved 'situation': position, place, or circumstances.

In about 90 per cent of the times that 'situation' is used it is either unnecessary or placed where other words are equally applicable. Personally, I even go to the extreme of putting a red editorial pen through the word whenever I see it on a page. In a few instances I then reinstate it, for it turns out to be needed, and is the right word in the context. Often, though, it is used when the writer is too lazy to stop and think if there is a more precise word to convey the meaning. (See ABSTRACT WORDS.)

SIX Ws

The six Ws are the six words you need to have consciously in mind, to think about, and to have some answers to before you begin writing anything (although one of the six is really an H). These words are:

1 *Who* are you writing to (your reader)?

2 *Why* are you writing (what you hope to achieve, your purpose, and your task – in that order)?

3 *What* will you be writing (the content, including detail, level, and angle)?

4 & 5 *Where* and *when* will your document be read (to help you focus on length and layout)?

6 *How* will you write and present it?

Between them these six words will help you through the first phase of the writing cycle (see Figure 1) ie the thinking you need to do and the questions that need to be answered before you can write anything coherent. (See THINK; KNOWLEDGE; FACTS AND FIGURES.)

SPELLING

Spelling is more important than may appear at first glance. Why, you may ask, does it matter if you misspell a word or two? It doesn't change the meaning of what you're saying. Normally it doesn't, of course, but at times it does. For example, a common confusion exists between 'principal' and 'principle'. But misspelt words annoy the reader. Bad spelling indicates a 'why bother' attitude on the part of the writer, and this may get translated in the reader's mind to a 'who cares' attitude about the content. If a writer can't be bothered to spell correctly – or to check if they are unsure – the reader may begin to wonder if the 'can't be bothered to check the spelling', 'don't care' attitude spills over into 'can't be bothered to check the facts' or some other aspect of the document.

This may sound far-fetched, but it is a risk. Equally importantly, misspelling detracts from the ease of reading. At its worst, bad spelling results in an unprofessional job, in the same way that an incoherent structure or sloppy layout will.

Most word processing packages these days have spell-checks built into them, so there is no excuse for spelling mistakes.

SPIDER DIAGRAMS (see MIND-MAPS)

STORY – OR JOURNEY

Everything you write is, in a sense, a story. There is a beginning, a middle, and an end. Even if it is a simple memo asking someone to do something it needs a structure, like any story. So the beginning might be the reason you want something done differently; the middle would be what is happening now, and what needs to be done differently; the end is how this can be achieved.

As with any story you need to think about what is crucial to its telling and what superfluous; what adds a dimension to it and what detracts. One way of deciding what is vital and what irrelevant is to draw three circles (see Figure 5).

Figure 5
The three circles of relevance

As with any story, once more, you need to engage your reader by having a punchy BEGINNING, using action-laden language if appropriate, varying your sentence structure and length, and sticking to the point of the 'story'.

If you think of everything you write as being a type of story, you may find your texts become more alive and more coherent. (See FEELING STUCK?)

STRUCTURE

A structure such as a building is something solid and fixed. A boat, a building, a cup . . . all have a particular shape. They are shapes into which something has to be fitted. Structures of written material may also come into this category. Indeed many organisations have preset formats (structures) for reports or other common documents. Many of these structures make good sense for a reader and make writing them easier too. A series of documents with the same structure or pattern will often be easy for readers, who can anticipate what is in them, and readily find specific information within them.

There are some standard structures for documents such as REPORTS. Even MEMOS can follow a given structure. Letters are more complex, for each one is different, but there are some general elements to remember (see LETTERS).

But structures may also sometimes act as a strait-jacket. A writer following a structure may not think of certain elements that are nonetheless important – simply because there is no heading for them in the fixed structure. So if you suddenly have some inspiration, or an idea which doesn't fit into the established pattern, you may well lose them.

Treat structures with a certain caution. For some they may kill off creativity; for others they may be the stimulus for it. My preference is to work with a looser OUTLINE until the final structure is ready to emerge. (See LOGIC AND LINKING.)

STYLE

Not surprisingly people use 'style' to mean different things: it is a classic ABSTRACT WORD! I use it here to mean the way in which the 'message' of the text is expressed (ie not the content or the STRUCTURE). Therefore the style of a text includes:

- whether it was written in a formal or conversational way
- the general tone (forceful, confused, angry)
- the use of language (the vocabulary, grammar)
- the RHYTHM AND FLOW
- the appearance and LAYOUT
- your own inimitable way of expressing yourself.

Think of writing style as akin to styles of guitar playing: jazz or classical, folk or rock. The essential instrument doesn't change, but the playing of it does. Or take painting: you can (if you're interested in painting!) recognise and distinguish between a Mondrian or a Michelangelo, a Van Gogh or a van Eyck. (See WRITING IS CREATING.)

The style of a document tells a reader a great deal about you, the writer, and your general awareness of how to communicate with others.

We each speak differently – with a different tone of voice, different vocabulary. We are (we hope) truly ourselves when we speak and act. Because writing is simply another way of relating to others, our own style will therefore emerge, and be important – but to what degree will depend on whether, when we write, we are representing a department or section, or just ourselves. If the former, we may need to modify our personal style. But there will be occasions when we need to be ourselves, also. (See BE YOURSELF; CLONING.)

FORMAL OR CONVERSATIONAL

As I have said elsewhere in this book, we write different kinds of letter to our grandmother, our boss, our child, or our lover. This is true not just in terms of the content but also of the way our message is conveyed. Is it a loose string of ideas simply flung down on paper, as unstructured as a conversation; or is it something well thought-out, with headings? Is the language colloquial, everyday language, or rather more polished?

A formal letter might begin 'Dear Mr So-and-so'; an informal one 'Dear Jo'. A memo to a colleague might omit the 'Dear' and start simply with the person's name, and go straight to the point.

We might write, informally, 'I'm sending the article for you to read', or we might fall into the formality and say, 'I am sending the enclosed for your perusal.'

We might write to some people, in a casual way, 'Did

you get my letter?' A more formal version might be, 'I hope you received my letter.' Which is the more appropriate is up to you to decide, depending on whom you are writing to and your purpose in so doing.

If you can't decide how formal or informal to be ask someone – someone who has experience of writing to the same person, or whose judgement you can trust.

FACTUAL OR DISCURSIVE

When writing, you need to have some idea what type of text your readers might prefer. Will they respond best to facts and figures or to intuitive statements and possibilities; do they prefer categorical statements or 'maybes'? What follows here is a list of opposites to consider

facts	– *ideas*
practical solutions	– *possibilities*
logic and reasoning	– *values and beliefs*
words	– *visual material*
sticking to the subject	– *digressions*
cut and dried	– *space for development of ideas*
judgement and conclusions	– *'maybes'*
impersonal style	– *personal style*
certainties	– *questions*
analysis	– *intuition*
familiar, safe, and routine	– *pioneering, risky, and creative*

Knowing what your readers like (which is difficult if there are many) means being better able to give them what they will find helpful and useful.

GENERAL TONE AND LANGUAGE

The tone of any document lies in its expressiveness and other qualities of language. Is it for instance forceful and determined or confused and ill thought-out? These, and other characteristics, will come across in the language the writer uses, and in how logical and well-ordered the text is.

If words are used precisely and an argument is thought-out and ordered well, the reader will gain an impression of a clear-thinking writer. The general layout and presentation will add to this impression. Where words are used imprecisely, thoughts do not follow one another logically, and the layout is messy the reader will gain the opposite impression.

SUMMARIES

A summary is a stand-alone document. It is, as the word implies, a précis or brief account of a longer document. It is a stand-alone document because summaries – which are usually short, one- or two-page documents – are sent to (often senior) people who are interested in knowing the outcome of some work but do not require to know the details of how it was reached. All they need is a summary.

Because of the target audience and purpose a summary's structure is important. While summaries contain the essence of each part of a longer document or REPORT their contents may not be in the same order as the original document's. This is because the readers of summaries are usually interested in results, outcomes, conclusions, recommendations, or suggestions. So, after outlining – probably in no more than two or three sentences – why the work and subsequent report were originally undertaken the next thing is to state, upfront, what the results, insights, or recommendations are. (See UPSIDE-DOWN REPORTING).

To get an insight into how other writers do this read the opening paragraphs of articles in such publications as *The Economist* or *New Scientist.* Their writers encapsulate the ESSENCE of a piece of work very well.

The structure of a summary may then look something like this:

- the purpose/prompt/issue/possibility/challenge
- the outcomes/results/findings/insights/ideas
- possibly some background
- the recommendations, actions, etc that should follow in some summaries (this point may follow on after the outcomes have been listed)
- a synopsis of what was done to reach the results and conclusions
- information on how to get hold of the whole document (if the summary is not attached to it).

As the last bullet point implies such summaries may be attached to the whole document within the first few introductory pages. The reader then has the choice of reading the full text, or just the summary. Alternatively summaries may be sent to people who have no need, or possibly even interest, in seeing the whole document. They can nonetheless be told how and where to find it, should they want to.

If a document is on a technical – or in some way difficult – subject a non-technical summary for 'laypeople' is a very useful adjunct to the whole. In such instances the summary may well be longer than the two pages (or fewer) specified earlier.

T

TABLE OF CONTENTS

If your document is going to run to more than five or six pages readers will find a table of contents very helpful. You need to list the main headings along with the page numbers on which they are to be found. If you have a number of smaller headings in your text do not list them all but decide which level of headings would most help readers find their way around.

If the document has appendices and a bibliography they should appear on the contents page as well. And if it has figures, tables, and other visual material these can also be listed in a separate table or list of figures.

Tables of contents giving page numbers cannot, of course, be finally prepared until the document is at the proof-reading stage, for page numbers may change up till that point.

TAUTOLOGY

A tautology occurs when what is said or written contains an unnecessary 'repetition'. Examples of common tautologies are:

- a new innovation (an innovation cannot by definition be old)
- a period of time (period means a space in time)
- in close proximity (proximity is by definition close)

- ✦ the true facts (as opposed to the untrue ones?)
- ✦ in my own personal opinion (your personal opinion can only be your own)
- ✦ in equal halves (halves are always equal)
- ✦ superimposed over each other (superimposed includes the sense of 'over')
- ✦ enclosed with this . . . ('enclosed' includes the notion of 'with')
- ✦ totally impossible (impossible means impossible)
- ✦ conclusive proof (proof is by definition conclusive)
- ✦ almost unique (either it is or it is not unique)
- ✦ the other alternative ('alternative' means the other choice)

Using tautologies indicates to readers that you don't know the meaning of words you are using. A dictionary may help!

THESAURUS

A thesaurus – a compilation of synonyms and closely related words and phrases – is indispensable for a writer. It helps you choose the most appropriate word for a sentence, offers an instant variety of synonyms when you want to vary the words you are using, and enlarges your vocabulary, making your written document vastly more interesting for your readers – always a bonus!

The English language is vast and varied. It contains words that express the slightest nuance and difference. Choosing the right one can be crucial to meaning and interpretation. The greater the variety of words in any text you write, the more interesting it is for a reader. Repetitious vocabulary leads not only to boredom but also means that a reader is more likely to want to miss out chunks of your text, particularly if skimming through it, or interrupted as they read.

On the other hand you may have a sound reason for repeating certain words. They sound like gongs for a reader, and make sure a particular point is made. And if you've been asked to write about a certain subject you may in fact have little choice but to repeat. However, be aware of the dangers of too much repetition.

THINK Before you start writing, you need to think about, and find answers to, the following six questions:

1 Whom are you writing your document for?

2 Why you are writing it?

3 What do you need to put in it?

4 & 5 Where and when will your reader be using or reading it?

6 How will you write and present your material?

These are the SIX Ws, and form the first stage in the writing cycle (see Figure 1). Without answers to them you will find it difficult to write and focus your document. Being clear about them, and keeping them in your conscious mind as you write, is immensely helpful, for you can keep checking that your material is relevant and focused.

If you don't know the answers to some of the six questions ask someone, get the information you need to make you confident you are addressing the right person, with the right material. If you don't know the answers your confusion will show through in the writing. The reader will detect it instantly. Woolly thinking leads to woolly writing . . .

WHOM YOU ARE WRITING FOR?

Who, in fact, is your reader? It is obviously crucial to know who your audience is, for it affects your content and how you present the document. (See READERS: WHO ARE THEY?)

WHY YOU ARE WRITING?

This is a question with many layers to it. It needs to be broken down into three elements: the outcome ie the end result to which your report is contributing; next, what prompted it; and third, what you need to give your readers ie they have needs which it is your task to meet. (See WHY ARE YOU WRITING?)

WHAT WILL YOU WRITE?

This refers to the content of your document, be it a letter, memo, or report, and is determined by your answers to the two previous questions. It covers not simply the subject matter but reminds you of your 'task'. So if your task is to give information, how much do you give, what level of detail, how complex or simple does it need to be, does it need a particular angle? If your task is to make recommendations you need to have thought out your explanations, give evidence backing them, list benefits, and so on. (See KNOWLEDGE; WHY ARE YOU WRITING?)

WHERE AND WHEN WILL YOUR DOCUMENT BE USED OR READ?

Knowing this helps you primarily to decide how to present your material. BRIEFING NOTES for a meeting will require a different layout, spacing, and highlighting than, say, a letter to be read at a desk. Similarly if your boss is going to a meeting in a day or two's time there is little point in giving him a 60-page report to read; instead he needs a SUMMARY.

HOW WILL YOU CONVEY – AND WRITE – YOUR MATERIAL?

This 'how' refers in fact to two things: the first is the medium you will use, the second is the appropriate language and presentation.

The 'medium' refers to whether you will send a letter, a memo, or an E-mail, whether you will write a report on some work you have done, or decide on a presentation with brief notes. You may not have a choice of medium, but if you do, consider which is most appropriate.

The second 'how' refers to the language, the general STYLE and the LAYOUT. These in turn are determined by who your readers are: are they familiar with your JARGON and the subject matter, or do you need to explain everything in layman's terms? And what about using VISUAL MATERIAL to back up the WORDS?

THOUGHTS

Thoughts often lie hidden in our minds, and we may be unaware of them. They emerge as we begin to write. Thoughts you never knew you had might suddenly begin to spill out onto the page or screen. This is one of the great advantages of writing things down. It's probably something to do with getting our minds into gear, so that they begin thinking for us, so to speak, making the process of writing almost effortless. One thought leads on to another, and at times it may feel as though someone else is directing what we write! Something similar occurs when we are asked to tell someone about something. We begin by thinking we have nothing to say, but as we speak, more and more emerges. (See FEELING STUCK?)

A TIME AND PLACE TO WRITE

If we want our texts to be good, elegant, readable, and of a high quality, we need to create time and space to write. 'Impossible,' I hear many readers mutter. Well, the quality of the writing will reflect the lack of priority given to these two factors.

We've seen, in the introduction to this book, that writing is at least as important, if not more so, than the spoken words in our everyday contacts with people. What is written remains for others to reread, to comment on at leisure, and to criticise minutely in a way that the spoken word doesn't allow. The spoken word is blown away, and we remember only the gist of the messages, not the individual words spoken.

What we write leaves us open to be judged on our ability to think clearly, to express ourselves succinctly, and to have our readers' interests ever in our minds. So we owe it to ourselves, and indeed to the section, department, or organisation on whose behalf our document is being written, to make quality time to produce good texts. Each section, department, or organisation will be judged by the final products of each writer.

As more and more people have 'written communication' as one of the competencies they have to show, maybe it will be easier to get that quality time. To produce the best, we need to be given the opportunity to do so, as with any other competency we hope to gain.

Many businesses, however, still underestimate the activity of writing – while laying great stress on the excellence of the final product! But the final product is – and can only be – a reflection of the importance given to the time it takes to write, and whether it is written in a place without interruptions or in noisy offices with phones ringing and colleagues talking.

Few writers, even great literary figures, produce written material as if it simply fell off a production line. Writing is a more organic, creative activity (see WRITING IS CREATIVE). So what does this mean in practice?

It means not being interrupted. It means making it clear that the writing is a priority – at least for a few hours. It means having somewhere to be able to concentrate and focus, preferably somewhere quiet. This is particularly so when writing longer and complex documents that need to have a thread holding them together, to have some coherence and consistency.

Some organisations do now have 'quiet rooms' equipped with word processors; others allow people with larger documents to prepare to work from home for half- or full days.

TITLES

Titles are the first thing that readers will look at, whether the document you have sent them is a report, memo, or E-mail. The title is the main way of SIGNPOSTING for readers whether the document is worth reading. Will it be relevant for them? Will they be interested? Will it tell them what they are looking for, or something new?

Think about yourself as a reader. Have you ever looked at titles and tried to guess what is in a document only to find that, when you read it, the document is not really about what you thought? The title was misleading. Often the problem is that titles don't tell us enough. So a misleading title will either waste a reader's time or put off a document people who would really gain from or be interested in what it has to say. And all because of the title!

These problems usually arise if titles are made up of four or five nouns strung together with no verbs to show how they relate to one another. Such verbless titles have no life about them, no sense of energy. They do not convey what direction the document is going in. They are deadheads!

So how do you create more interesting titles? Well, one way is to think about, and say out loud, what the document is really about. What is its ESSENCE? What is its main finding? That should give you some clues. Second, you might consider putting a question into a title, maybe as a second part to it: for instance, 'Training adults: how do different ways of learning affect the design of programmes?'

Another useful way to tackle a title (or what might come under the heading of 'Subject' or 'Purpose' if it is a memo) is to state upfront what you hope to achieve. This could be an eye-catcher. For instance, consider this title: 'Computer card processing.' This tells you nothing about what is in the memo, or why it is being sent. However, 'Changing the computer card procedure' begins to give us clues. 'How to improve the information on computer cards' may give yet more clues, and so on. Using a verb (even in a foreshortened form) in a title helps readers to understand the thrust of the document.

There are endless possibilities for making business titles (and even memo 'Purposes') more interesting and in particular more enlightening for the reader. It's all part of the FRONTLOADING that so much business writing still fails to do.

TONE

(see STYLE)

TRAINING MATERIALS

Training materials differ depending on whether they are to be used as, say, exercises in a workshop or during a course, for distance learning, or whether they are to be taken away by participants at the end of a programme for reference.

In all cases, however, before preparing such materials you need to be clear what outcome you hope will be achieved by the students/participants using them. If you can say what you hope they will be able to do it will keep you focused on making sure the material you produce achieves just that.

Whatever materials are prepared they need to have a professional appearance and be typed out. Some diagrams may be hand-drawn but should also look neat and tidy. Materials should be written and laid out in a consistent style, if possible, and be bound together simply or placed in a loose-leaf folder.

To illustrate the two main types of training materials – those for use during a course or workshop, and those given as handouts – let me give a few brief examples of materials for a writing workshop I would run. (Distance learning material, however, is of a different quality, because 'students' use it on their own. Writing distance learning material is a skill in itself, and this is not the place to go into it, nor is there the space.)

OVERHEAD PROJECTORS

I use overhead projectors, or OHPs, as guides for myself and the participants during a workshop. I prepare transparencies for such OHPs for all the main elements of writing. Each has on it key words only, or a key diagram. In a workshop I would use the Writing Cycle (see Figure 1) either to talk generally about how I propose to work systematically on a two-day workshop or to pinpoint – after discussing a participant's blocks and problems, and looking at a few examples of their written work – where their difficulties seem to lie eg whether at the thinking or writing stage.

Having OHP transparencies on the main elements of writing means they can be either used in a logical way ie on a tutor-led course or pulled out whenever participants ask a question and want to work on a particular issue. So if the issue being discussed was 'Paragraphs' I would display the relevant OHP transparency, which would have on it a few key phrases such as:

- ✦ one idea, one paragraph; new idea, new paragraph.
- ✦ no more than 100 words in a paragraph.
- ✦ link paragraphs.

The points on an OHP transparency need to be brief, but they raise talking points, and give participants a chance to look at their own written work brought to the workshop in the light of the points on the OHP.

HANDOUT EXERCISES

Exercises are a form of handout, but in my workshops they are geared to specific points I am trying to make, or aspects of writing I want participants to practise. This may be done by participants during the workshop, possibly before it, or between the first and second day of a two-day workshop. Such exercises need clear explanations so that participants know what is expected of them. They should also be told how their work will be used, or assessed (if this is the case).

After discussing active and passive verbs with them, for example, I might ask participants to rewrite sentences on the handouts that have used the passive form of the verb into ones using the active form. Alternatively I might ask them to put into their own words (to paraphrase) a short text I have written, then to share their versions with others, and see that there is no one way of writing something. Another option is for me to give participants a text to précis ie to extract the essential message of the text.

HANDOUTS TO TAKE AWAY

Handouts to take away will expand on several of the main points that occur on the OHP transparencies only as key words. Because they are used in a different way – ie by a reader, on his or her own, before or after the workshop – they need this extra detail in them. For such handouts I might use some of the texts in this book. So, for instance, handouts on REPORTS or SUMMARIES might not differ very much from the text here.

An alternative is to give participants copies of the OHP transparencies at the beginning of the workshop and allow them to write down the points they want to ie whatever is particularly relevant for them.

DISTANCE LEARNING MATERIAL

Distance learning material would combine all of the above types of material, but would differ from those used in a workshop. Whereas, during a workshop, material can be used in random ways to work with whatever participants need 'here and now', distance learning material has to be very clearly and logically structured to allow people to work on their own. It would therefore be a step-by-step progression through the writing cycle.

After explaining the cycle the material would focus on each stage, use the equivalent of OHP transparencies to highlight the main points, give longer explanatory texts on various other points, and link all of this with practical exercises. The participants would need to carry out these exercises before moving on to the next step in the material.

To give it a sense of reality such a written programme might take a writer through a text they are actually having to write, so they end up with a final, polished document.

TYPEFACES, TYPESIZES

The word typeface refers to the 'design' of the letters and figures in the alphabet eg Times, Baskerville, Plantin – each of which has the full range of roman and italic variations. This book, for example, is set in a typeface called Garamond for the main text; the headings are in a different typeface, called Futura Book.

Using different typefaces and typesizes is a way of making the text look more interesting – simply because there is variation. Such differences also help a reader through the different parts of any text, because it distinguishes them.

The most common font in each typeface is the medium roman, which is used for the bulk of everyday texts. Bold (ie heavy type) and italics are used for emphasis and to create distinctions.

Typesizes vary from tiny to vast. The texts of most documents are printed out in a size called 10 pt (point) or 12 pt (this text is actually in 9 pt, but you do not need to understand how these sizes are arrived at). What this means is that main and important headings need to be larger than the size of the main text, and probably in bold, whereas less important headings can be in italics or the same face as the text, and even the same size.

So, different faces and sizes help for instance to distinguish different headings in a text. The only thing a writer needs to beware of is consistency in their use. If a major section heading appears in a particular typeface and typesize, that one must be used consistently through the text. One way of checking the relevant levels of heading is to go back to – or create – a MIND-MAP which will indicate the relative levels.

Different typefaces can also highlight different sorts of text; for example, quotations are often set in italics. There is also a convention to set the titles of books in italics.

If you have never stopped to think about this element of a document, look at magazines, books, and brochures as well as documents produced in your own organisation to get ideas on how to use typefaces and typesizes.

QUOTE/UNQUOTE

"*To do our work we all have to read a mass of papers. Nearly all of them are far too long. This wastes time, while energy has to be spent in looking for the essential points.*"

Sir Winston Churchill (1874–1965)

UPSIDE-DOWN REPORTING

For much of our education, whether it is writing essays or carrying out experiments, we are taught to write in a deductive way. We begin with a description or we outline what we plan to do. Then we proceed to build up step by step to the great climax, the 'hey presto' factor: we have a result, an insight, a need to do something differently.

In business writing, we need to reverse this process. Although our *thinking* will still be deductive we need to convey the opposite in our *writing*. We should begin with our discoveries, our ideas, what we need to be doing, then state the benefits or advantages, and then – if relevant to our audience – describe how we arrived at our conclusions. (See FRONTLOADING.)

USE YOUR CRITICAL JUDGEMENT

Most of us are critical readers. We know when something is good, adequate, or poor. We know when a document holds our attention or frustrates us. We know when it's difficult to find our way around it. There is value in stopping to analyse, when we come across such a document, what exactly is 'wrong' with it. This will increase our critical judgement of our own texts.

We may already be subconsciously aware of what's

wrong: our GUT FEELINGS often let us know. But to change and improve, we need first to become more critically aware, then be able to pinpoint what is wrong, and finally to have some ideas on how to revise the text. So is it our language, our logic (or lack of it), the structure (or lack of it), the layout, or what?

Read your own work as though it were someone else's. Would it satisfy you? If you find this difficult to do, persist. Eventually you'll be able to tell if it will read well and convince another reader.

QUOTE/UNQUOTE

"*A good sentence is like a fine meal: something you want to relish.*"

Anon.

V

VARIETY

Variety is the spice in writing. Varying the way your write – whether it's how you begin sentences, how you construct them, or the words you use – creates interest.

When you're writing about something you have done (a report of a visit, maybe) avoid starting every sentence with 'I'.There are endless ways of beginning sentences. Vary also the length and rhythm of your sentences, If they are all approximately the same length a sense of routine sets in for the reader. So add surprise. Use a few short, punchy sentences followed by longer ones. Choose the short ones to make a point and the longer ones to explain it, for instance. And vary the words you use. A THESAURUS is an excellent way of finding words with the same meaning, or one so close you are able to use it.

VERBS

Verbs are the energy in sentences: they drive them forward, if they're allowed to! Active verbs create movement; passive ones, by contrast, pull backwards. The passive is slow and formal, but worst of all it often avoids the issue of responsibility and accountability.

Compare 'It was decided [passive] to remove all signs from the roads' with 'The local authority's traffic department decided [active] to remove all signs from the roads.' In the first sentence people responsible and accountable for doing something are unidentified; in the second you know whom to phone. If you were determined to stick with the passive voice you could of course write, 'It was decided by the local authority's traffic department to remove all signs from the roads', but this is very clumsy. Plans get implemented, decisions taken, systems agreed to – but the shadowy figures who do all this implementing, deciding, and agreeing are not identified.

Passive verbs are however beloved of businesses and scientists. The latter conventionally use the passive when describing scientific experiments or research and its results. Businesses, though, have little reason to use it but do so, I suspect, because it has a more formal ring, results in longer SENTENCES (which many think add weight to an argument), and give the impression of having had more work put into them than straightforward sentence patterns or active verbs. Because businesses have been using this form for years there is a feeling that this is the only way to write! Yet we tend to use the active form of verbs when we speak. So it's patently acceptable to do the same when we write.

What then are the advantages of the active verb? For a start, it results in shorter sentences. And if one of our aims, when improving our writing, is to make documents shorter and snappier this is a good way of achieving just that! Second, the active form pinpoints responsibilities. We have to name the person or people carrying out an action, taking a decision, coming to an agreement. Third, it makes for easier and more 'reader-friendly' texts, because it resembles conversation.

There will of course be times when the passive form is needed, and using the active would make no sense. This is particularly so in scientific writing, where it would be pointless to describe a project in terms of 'I did such and such' – because it is not the actions, but the results, that matter. As for you non-scientists, however: think when you use the passive form whether it is really necessary, or whether you are using it because, in your opinion, it sounds more impressive?

VISUAL MATERIAL

'A picture speaks a thousand words.' This statement reminds us that visual images stay in the mind longer than a string of words. A visual representation of what you are trying to say will not only enhance your text: your readers are more likely to remember the point. We ignore the visual at our peril! Our visual ability lies in the right side of our brain, and hence using it increases our ability to think and act.

We are living at present in a society which is highly visually-oriented – with television, newspaper photographs, advertisements. We expect visual material.

There are many advantages to using visual material. It makes a text more attractive at first glance. It creates interest. Try it out for yourself: do you find, when flicking through a document, that you stop and look at the visual material, rather than read the text?

So what are the possibilities? There are photos and drawings, flow charts, pie charts and bar charts. Tables are not really visual material. They are simply another block of text, often difficult to decipher unless you pinpoint what it is you want your reader to note. You can do this by visual means (even a 'finger' pointing to the appropriate figures).

Of course the other way to create a visual impact, if you aren't able to use visual material, is to use layout and spacing. This is one reason for the popularity of 'white space' – it allows the eye to travel more easily through a text.

You can achieve other visual effects by using bullet points, by making sure the text is split into several paragraphs, and by using different typefaces and typesizes (though not too many). Another option is to create, say, two columns of text rather than one block of it. Shorter lines are sometimes easier to read or scan than one long line.

If it is especially important that a text has great visual impact it is worth asking a book designer to create a layout for you, particularly for longer or more important documents. You will then have a template to follow in subsequent documents.

WHERE TO START?

The first thing to say is: you don't have to begin at the beginning with the introduction and work methodically, even mechanically, through to the end. In fact introductions can be the most difficult part to write, and are often best left to the end!

There is no one best way of starting, and you can start anywhere. You may want to start with your conclusions. Or you may find it is easiest to write some descriptive bits of your document. Writing what you know best is another way to begin.

Everyone has their own preference, and each approach is as good as the next. What you do need to do, though, is to make sure that before you go too far you stop and think about an OUTLINE and the logical ordering of your thoughts. You also need to stop and consider the SIX Ws – in particular, why you're writing, and whom for. If you don't, you may find that what you have already written is not relevant. On the other hand if it has released your thinking and given you a sense of direction then it may not matter that your first efforts are destined for the wastebasket or deletion from the word processor! (See also FEELING STUCK?; MIND-DUMPING; THINK.)

WHY ARE YOU WRITING?

Asking yourself why you are writing the text you are about to undertake is vital. It is one of the SIX Ws that make up the thinking process you need to go through before you write anything. It is also a useful reminder once you begin to write, for it keeps you on track.

This question can be broken down into three elements:

1 the outcome ie the end result to which your report is contributing
2 what prompted it
3 what you need to give your readers – they have needs which it is your task as the writer to meet.

A model of what you need to focus on here may illustrate these points better than just words. It will show the distinction between the outcome; the readers' needs; the writer's task; and the prompt (see Figure 6).

Figure 6
The steps for focused writing

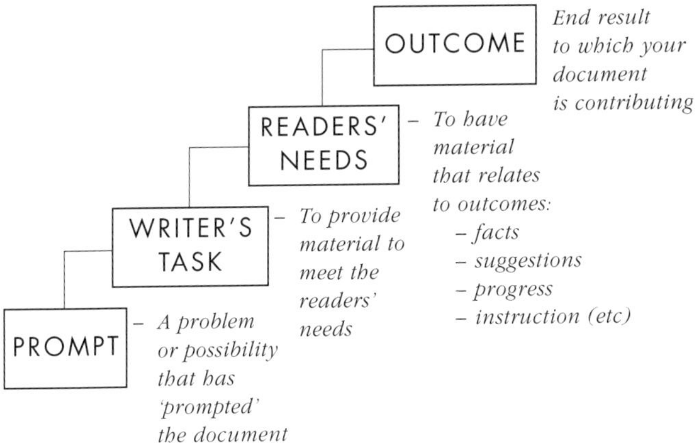

OUTCOME

Before I can write a really focused document I need to know what my readers will be doing, be able to do, or be contributing to after they've had my document: decisions, actions? This will help me understand their needs better (particularly if they've not told me what those needs are!) and ensure I meet them. So if I'm writing about a training process, is it because my readers will themselves have to run a particular programme, or because they just need to know about it? If the former, their needs – and my task – are not the same as when they just need to know about it.

Being clear about the outcome means you are better able to FRONTLOAD your document, to say at the very beginning what you want your reader to do; or to draw out the essence of your document; or to state clearly what you hope or expect your document to achieve. Being clear about all of this also gives you an opening statement for your INTRODUCTION, particularly if it is to a longer report.

READERS' NEEDS

In the light of the outcome I can now begin to be more specific about my readers' needs: a need to understand, to have the facts, to be given various options and the advantages and disadvantages of each, and so on.

WRITER'S TASK

Readers' needs give a writer a clear focus for his or her own task. It may be to give information, to list options, to assess alternatives, to describe a process, and so on. Their needs also help a writer to decide on the content of the document, the angle, the detail, what will be relevant, and so on.

THE PROMPT

The prompt may be a past or existing problem or issue; it may equally be some future possibilities or challenges. Being aware of the prompts (which feed directly into the hoped-for outcome, of course) also gives the writer a clearer focus.

Being clear about the answers to all these points also helps when creating, first, an outline and then a final structure to a document.

WORDS

Words are the tools of writing. They are our chief means of communicating with our fellow human beings (the other means being visual symbols and body language).

We may never be sure of having managed to communicate exactly what we want. But we can try to be as clear and precise as possible. Indeed we need to, for, since MEANING IS IN PEOPLE, imprecise and vague words lead to misunderstandings.

Words – and hence phrases or whole sentences – are rather like boats. They convey, as their passengers, a writer's or speaker's meaning. And just as there are a variety of boats, so the way that words are put together will also differ. Some will be slow and ponderous, like aircraft carriers; others will be light and airy, like sailing-boats riding over the crest of the waves; others are sturdy, simple, and workmanlike*, like rowing-boats.

The aircraft carriers are abstract words, clichéd phrases, and complex sentences whose meaning is often obscure. The

* *This is an example of what many would call a 'sexist' word. I have deliberately left it in; but see* X-ORCISE THE -ISMS *for reasons why we need to be more aware of the messages sent by using sexist, racist, or other discriminatory expressions.*

writer whose verbal fleet consists solely of these is patently trying to impress, not express.

The sailing-boats that skim over the waves are words and phrases with little weight or meaning, although they may convey striking images and appeal to our imagination. They often have an elegance that is simply pleasing or even amusing (as in the language of advertising).

The workmanlike rowing boats are the words that are the simplest and often shortest way of conveying what we mean. There will be little confusion in texts that use them, but they may read rather starkly and lack elegance.

Good writing will not stick exclusively to any one way of conveying meaning. It will 'mix and match' ('mix and match' is a sailing-boat phrase!) because to add variety is interesting. The clue is to know what you're doing and why you're choosing certain words and phrases. You need to become aware of how you're expressing yourself.

WRITE LIKE YOU SPEAK

This message appears in many entries in this alphabet. Writing is a dialogue with your readers. Your words create a 'bridge' between yourself and them. If you find this difficult, try pretending, as you write, that a reader is sitting opposite you, and you are speaking to them, telling them something. Your language will be much freer and more direct if you do this. And the more you write as if you were having a conversation, the easier you will find the task of writing, and the clearer your texts will be.

There is of course a caveat. We don't always speak grammatically; we don't always finish sentences; we use jargon and abbreviations. But we convey our meaning clearly – most of the time. When speaking we rarely fall into the trap of formality, or weighty words and sentences.

So why do we not heed this and express ourselves in writing as we do in speech? There are probably many reasons. At school we were told it was incorrect to use everyday phrases and informal speech. The marks given for our essays highlighted this. At work, these same old myths persist. They have grown into beliefs that this is the way to write. Everyone expects this (or so the beliefs claim) – even though you (and every other writer) may always have felt uncomfortable writing in this way.

Readers have also been left feeling just as puzzled. Why this long-windedness when the writing could be more straightforward, and get to the point more directly?

In sociology this behaviour has a name: the Abilene syndrome. The analogy is of a three-generation family: grandparents, children/parents, and grandchildren. The children/parents feel they should take their parents (ie the grandparents) out for a day, to Abilene, some 100 miles away, although they themselves would prefer to stay at home. The grandparents would likewise prefer to stay at home and enjoy playing with the grandchildren, but think the children/parents want to go to Abilene. The grandchildren are told that they have to go to Abilene for the day, even though they also would prefer to stay at home and play. And so all six set out for a day in Abilene, which none of them wants, and yet no one will voice this concern.

So it is with business writing: everyone produces texts in a style that they think everyone else wants but they personally don't. No one, however, wants or dares express their unhappiness both at having to write in this way and having to read material thus written. The veil of silence persists.

WRITING IS CREATING Writing is like painting a picture or composing music. It is an act of creating.

Each of us, like artists or composers, have our own way of writing, just as we have our own way of speaking. We may not be able fully to express this personal style when writing business documents. They have a certain format, formality of language, and a number of other conventions. But even within those each of us can, if we try, express ourselves. A text that comes from an individual rather than a 'clone' reads much better and is more persuasive and convincing.

That individuality comes across in the RHYTHM AND FLOW of our written language, in our preference for certain words, in the ENERGY we put into what we write. It can come across simply by putting more of ourselves into those written documents. (See CLONING; WRITE LIKE YOU SPEAK.)

The act of writing is also the fourth stage of the writing cycle (see Figure 1). It is the stage at which we put pen to paper (or finger on keyboard) in a more focused way than when we're trying first to organise our thoughts.

Don't feel however that you have to sit down and write a clean, logical text at the first attempt; or that you need to begin at the beginning and work your way through to the end. Most of us don't do either of these things. So although it is the writing stage it may still resemble more a mind-dump of thoughts and ideas which then need to be ordered logically (see MIND-DUMPING). And you can still start with whatever part of the document feels easiest, simply because the very act of beginning will get you into the flow of writing. (See FEELING STUCK?; WHERE TO START?)

Because writing is creative you also need to allow not only the logical processes to play their part; you need to allow your subconscious to do some work for you too, along with the creative right side of your brain. Be kind to yourself and take time out to go for a walk, make a cup of coffee, or even sleep on an idea. Giving the brain a break is really refreshing and helpful. (See A TIME AND PLACE TO WRITE.)

Don't feel that you need to have everything mapped out before you start writing. Few artists, potters, or musicians know exactly what will emerge when they start creating. Putting yourself in a strait-jacket may stop the creative juices flowing! Think of a loose-jointed OUTLINE instead. The logic can come later.

Of course, one way of improving your own writing is to read good writers. This alphabet is not the place to give examples of literary style, but writers such as Lawrence Durrell, Jane Austen, Malcolm Bradbury, Brian Keenan, Doris Lessing, Ernest Hemingway, Raymond Chandler, Sean O'Faolain, and Penelope Lively are each in their own way worth reading to note their different styles.

You could also read the editorials in newspapers; or choose journalists whose writing appeals to you – possibly Michael Frayn in the *Guardian*, Miles Kington in the *Independent*, or Bernard Levin in *The Times*. In the end there is no substitute for reading, and becoming critically aware of the fine writing styles of others. It is the best way of improving your own style.

X-ORCISE THE 'ISMS'

In writing, as in speech, you need to be aware of the 'isms' that creep into our everyday language, almost without our realising. The 'isms' are those things we say, or omit to say, relating to sexism, racism, ageism, and disablement. They include discriminatory phrases, generalisations, and omissions.

Each of them can harm and hurt those affected. They also affect adversely how others see, and the beliefs they hold about, those we discriminate against, categorise, generalise about, or omit altogether in our texts. When writing, we need to take care over both the form of our language and its contents.

LANGUAGE

The use of the masculine pronoun 'he' and the associated masculine endings to words, such as chairman, whereby half of the human population is ignored or omitted, is now widely viewed as unacceptable. Women prefer to be known as 'she', and texts need to be balanced accordingly. Footnotes saying that 'he' refers to everyone is not a happy solution. Where you have to refer to both sexes 'they' may be appropriate. Another possibility is to use 's/he'. But probably the best is to vary the use of 'he' and 'she'.

We also generalise about and categorise both men and

women, racial groupings, and the old. And we inadvertently humiliate the disabled by implying that they are all incapable. Thus, not all men are tough, ambitious, and achievers, nor are all women pretty and gentle. By a similar token, stereotyping in the opposite direction isn't acceptable either: the womaniser, the battleaxe. Women can be ambitious; men can be caring. Similarly the old are not always slow and incompetent. Nor do people of different races or nationalities all have the same characteristics eg 'fiery' Spaniards or 'lazy' Mexicans. And people with visual impairment don't have to 'tap their way' down the corridor. They can walk.

Make sure also, when talking about issues concerning the disabled, that you use the correct terminology. We no longer talk of 'the blind', but of people who have a 'visual impairment'; nor of 'the deaf', but of people who have a 'hearing disability'. This changed terminology more accurately describes the fact that these too are capable people who also happen to have a certain disability.

Language lays other traps for the unwary. The term 'black' is frequently used to denote things that are inherently bad, such as a 'black day', 'black economy' and 'blackleg'. Some find this unacceptable, because it links in some people's mind the notion that anything black, such as Black people, are by association also 'bad'. The opposite of this is the phrase 'lily-white', a possible inference being that 'Whites' are good.*

Other phrases also slip off the tongue. One such is 'industry has been crippled'; another is 'he doesn't have a leg to stand on'. Both of these may, for some, be offensive. A further example is 'younger members of staff are

* *While this book was being prepared, the Spastic Society changed its name to* Scope; *and in Chicago, some young Blacks have said they now prefer to be known as 'Niggers'.*

incapable of . . .', a phrase that may be as discriminatory and obviously untrue as phrases beginning 'All women . . .'.

Even such phrases as 'that's not cricket', although strictly speaking not discriminatory, may be incomprehensible to someone not brought up within the English education system. Likewise talk of 'second-generation immigrants' might cause resentment if the people in question were born in the UK. Be aware also that such words and expressions as 'chairman' and 'manpower planning' are potentially discriminatory. And what about 'managers and their wives'? Some managers have husbands . . .

These are just a few examples to make you more aware – if you are not already – of texts that may upset or anger readers.

CONTENT

Omission is as problematic as commission. If for instance you are writing training material you need to make sure that women, people of different races and nationalities, the disabled and the old are shown as active in responsible, professional, and managerial roles and not subservient ones. If you are preparing role-playing exercises make sure that the language and behaviours people are assigned aren't stereotyped; and that the ways in which people are described allow for variety.

In other texts – where you are reporting, say, on an assignment which involved interviewing people – make sure that your conclusions take everyone into equal account, and are not biased towards any one grouping.

If you are making proposals for a new course of action – maybe refurbishing offices – make sure that it is clear you have considered the needs of older or disabled members of staff. If you are preparing a paper on alternative and flexible working arrangements you should consider not just the possibilities of home-working or sharing office space but also take into account the needs of working or single parents, and propose alternatives for them such as crèches and flexitime.

In other words it is necessary to be aware of everyone's needs, not just those of the majority.

The same care, of course, needs to be taken with illustrations. Avoid stereotyping (eg men = managers, women = secretaries); and ensure that a mix of people – not just 'white male' – is shown.

QUOTE/UNQUOTE

> "*We should write one way to a strong man, another to a sluggard; one way to a green youth, another to an elder who has fulfilled his life; one way to a proud and successful man, another to a victim of adversity; one way to an enlightened literary scholar, another to one who can't grasp any high thoughts.*"
>
> Petrarch (1304–74)

YES OR NO?

When you're writing a text where you have to be clear that you are in favour of a particular action, want to accept a new idea, or think a particular suggestion helpful, say 'yes' clearly. If on the other hand you don't want to recommend a course of action, accept a suggestion or offer, or you think something is not a good idea, again be clear and say 'no'.

Beating about the bush, waffling, wrapping up what you want to say in long phrases, or punctuating your text with 'maybes', 'mights', and 'possibles' will leave your reader confused and probably irritated. Assertive writing is like assertive speaking: say things with conviction – unless, of course, you are genuinely unsure. Then express your uncertainty with equal clarity.

One good way of making sure you do say 'yes' or 'no' loud and clear is to create a heading in your text (probably one that you then delete before you send off your document) that *forces* you to be clear, eg 'So what do I really think?' (See COLOURS OF WRITING.)

Z

ZZZ... The letter 'z' is often used to show that someone is asleep. And this is what is intended here. There is positive value in sleeping on something you are writing, or having to write. During our sleep we often resolve questions or problems, have insights, or clear our minds of cobwebs and irrelevant intrusions. We even have the phrase, 'I need to sleep on it', normally applied to decisions or choices we need to make. But writing is full of decisions: what to say, how to say it, what to put in, what to leave out, and so on.

If you are someone who has brilliant ideas in the middle of the night you probably already have pencil and paper by the bedside to capture those elusive insights or answers which will certainly have otherwise flown by the time you get up.

So sleep on things that worry you when writing. This is simply another way of giving yourself space to think, just like making a cup of coffee, going for a walk, or doing some gardening. It's letting your brain do the work for you, without exerting too much effort yourself!

FURTHER READING

BARKER A. *The Right Report.* London, Industrial Society Press, 1993

BARRASS R. *Scientists Must Write.* London, Chapman and Hall, 1993

MILLER C. and SWIFT K. *Handbook of Non-sexist Writing.* London, The Women's Press, 1981

MINTO B. *The Pyramid Principle.* London, Pitman Publishing, 1991

STAUNTON N. *The Business of Communicating.* London, Pan, 1982

SWEETMAN S. *The Executive Memo.* Chichester, John Wiley and Sons, 1986

WAINWRIGHT G. *Successful Business Writing in a Week.* Sevenoaks, Hodder and Stoughton, 1993